W. M. (Wilber M.) Derthick

Studies in Musical History

An Educational Game of Composers, Musical Literature and....

W. M. (Wilber M.) Derthick

Studies in Musical History
An Educational Game of Composers, Musical Literature and....

ISBN/EAN: 9783337204860

Printed in Europe, USA, Canada, Australia, Japan

Cover: Foto ©Thomas Meinert / pixelio.de

More available books at **www.hansebooks.com**

STUDIES IN MUSICAL HISTORY.

· · ◀▶ · ·

Educational Game

· · · · · · ·

...OF...

...COMPOSERS, MUSICAL LITERATURE

...AND...

THE ELEMENTS OF CRITICISM.

o o O o o

AN INTELLECTUAL AND REFINED AMUSEMENT AND PROG-
RESS IN GENERAL MUSICAL KNOWLEDGE ACCORDING
TO A SYSTEMATICALLY GRADED COURSE.

o o O o o

DESIGNED AND PRACTICALLY DEVELOPED

—FOR THE—

MUSICAL STUDENTS AND AMATEURS,

BY W. M. DERTHICK,

Author of the "Manual of Music,"

. . ASSISTED BY . .

W. S. B. MATTHEWS,   A. J. GOODRICH,
J. VAN CLEVE,   SIGNOR E. DE CAMPI,
L. ELSON,   CALVIN B. CADY,
J. C. FILLMORE,   EMIL LIEBLING,
FREDERIC G. GLEASON,   AUBERTINE W. MOORE.

CHICAGO:
MANUAL PUBLISHING COMPANY,
415 DEARBORN STREET.

"I will point you out the right path of a pure and noble Education—laborious indeed at first ascent, but else so smooth and green and full of goodly prospects and melodious sounds on every side that the harp of Orpheus is not more charming."—MILTON.

INTRODUCTION.

In preparing the accompanying Studies in Musical History the author has endeavored to combine the pleasure of a refined amusement with a practical and efficien means of education. It is well known to educators tha the mind in its earlier stages of development is rarely disposed to serious and prolonged application, nor ever at a more advanced stage is it easily awakened to the at tentive contemplation of unfamiliar subjects. *Interest* i the first requisite to success in all study. How to arouse interest, thereby securing attention without effort, is the most important problem that presents itself to the teacher and to awaken the mind from its apathy and indifference and to divert its activities from idle and aimless pursuit into the "Elysian fields" of learning, is an object wel worthy the most ambitious effort. The principle in Froebel's philosophy, which renders his system of teach ing so successful, is that "the function of education is to develop the faculties *by arousing voluntary activity.*" This he accomplished by providing for his pupils "a graduated course of exercises modeled on the games in which he observed them to be most interested." In these games the acquisition of knowledge and the discipline o the mind were apparently made subservient to the grati fication of a natural desire for amusement; but the lessor was none the less lastingly inculcated, and the facultie pleasantly exercised, by these emulative and instructive exercises.

It is said of John Locke, author of the celebrated treatise upon "The Human Understanding," that the part of his advice which made most impression upon his contemporaries was his method of teaching reading and arithmetic by means of well considered games. The principle and the device are much older than these. Plato in his laws, speaking of Egypt, says: "In that country systems of calculation have actually been invented for the use of children, which they learn as a pleasure and an amusement. They have to distribute apples and garlands, adapting the same number to either a larger or a less number of persons; and they distribute to pugilists and wrestlers, or follow one another or they pair together by lot. Another method of amusing them is by taking vessels of gold and brass and silver and the like, and mingling them or distributing them without mingling. As I was saying, they adapt to their amusement the numbers in common use, and in this way make more intelligible to their pupils the arrangement and movement of armies and expeditions, and in the management of a household they make people more useful to themselves and wide-awake."—Jowett's Plato, "The Laws," p. 815.

Thus it would appear that the greatest educators and philosophers have chosen *games* as the most natural and efficient means of attracting the attention of students to subjects presenting at first little or no interest for them, and the success of such institutions, as the Kindergarten, fully demonstrates the practical effectiveness of this method.

The Studies herewith presented have grown out of the

character, as in the course of his contact with the musical public he has found that in spite of the vast amount of "taking lessons" in music, which exists in all parts of the country, there is little or no attention given to certain phases, which ought to enter into every study of music deserving the name. He refers to the history, and literature of music, and the principles of criticism, upon which alone a sound musical taste and intelligence can be founded. These subjects, so important, and so deeply interesting in themselves, are almost entirely neglected, and this not alone in the smaller centers, but even in the most important musical centers of the country. The average music student is profoundly ignorant of musical history and unversed in its literature.

If he is so fortunate as to make a practical acquaintance with certain compositions of one or more of the greater masters, the selections are detached, and learned, and forgotten as unrelated incidents; a piece by Beethoven, or Bach, or Chopin, standing in this respect but little different from one by Sidney Smith, or the popular writer of taking salon pieces of the day. Moreover, even if the student by reason of natural taste or good teaching should happen to prove an exception to this sweeping statement in the instance of one or even two sonatas of Beethoven, the two pieces stand detached still, and as a rule neither the pupil nor the teacher know whether the particular sonatas chosen represent the composer in his greater or lesser flights. Still less does the student conceive of the sonata as part of the manifold tone-poetry of the great master. In point of fact, there is much good reason for this deficiency, since in spite of the many books which have been written in this country concerning music, there is hardly one affording this information (unless the author be permitted to claim an exception in his *Manual of Music*, which was expressly written to fill this void.) Biographies we have, for students and for scholars, commentaries on the proper way of playing the greater works of the great masters, and many other excellent things for the aid of musical students; but the inquirer seeking for the best and representative works of the greatest masters will be driven to make up his selection unaided, or as the result of his own studies.

Still more noticeable is the difficulty if the student happen to desire to know which are the chief works of all the great composers in any one particular province of music. Here again he is driven to make his selection by guess. There is no work in which this information is found. In certain provinces, or more properly in certain side lights, there is indeed aid in several quarters, as for example in Mr. W. S. B. Matthews' "How to Understand Music," where the representative phases of music are discussed with considerable reference to this question in certain of its aspects; but it was not a part of the intention of that very popular and interesting work to answer the majority of the questions contained in the manual accompanying the present set of studies.

Much is said among amateurs concerning " sonatas " and "symphonies." Surely it is not a great deal to ask "Which are the greatest productions in these two departments of music?" Yet ask the first student one meets and the chances are that blank ignorance will be the discovery. "What are the leading chamber works?" Why is not this a valid question? Is not much said over and over again concerning the beauties of this department of music " Which are the great operas? Who were their composers? In what respects are these leading works alike, and in what different? What is the ideal of opera? What the ideal of chamber music? What is concerto, and how does it differ in form and character from chamber music? What is oratorio, and what are the greatest works of this kind? Wherein are these great works alike and wherein different? Would it be possible to compare their merits by a scale of valuations based upon their possessing or missing the most indispensable qualities of works of this kind?" Surely all these are legitimate questions. What is the chronological order of the greater composers? What are the principal forms in music? What is a fantasia? What are the greatest concertos? Who were the composers? Which concertos are best, and why? Is there anything unreasonable in such questions as these? What would be thought of a student of literature who found himself unable to give an approximate list of the greatest writers in the language in which he had been studying? Yet in music the corresponding knowledge is very rare. There are also many other questions which, although not so obvious, are nevertheless important. For example: What are the principles of the beautiful? What is meant by "classical" in music? What are the tests, which being passed, entitle a composition to this rank? What is "romantic" in music? The nomenclature of music contains many words of this character, signifying distinctions no less subtle than important; they are used daily by students and amateurs with no proper knowledge of their real meaning, and in connections which expose to silent criticism all those who thus ignorantly employ them. These are a few of the thousands of questions which are asked and answered in the Studies herewith, and answered in such a manner, with such clearness and definiteness, as to be easy to fix in the memory.

The information in the accompanying studies is sufficient to fill quite a good-sized volume. Let us consider it more in detail. The cards are arranged in classes, eight or sixteen cards in a class, according to the importance and magnitude of the subjects. There are sixteen cards devoted to the opera. Here, as in all other instances, the cards are of two kinds, general and special. The general cards are devoted to defining the qualities of the particular province of music to which they belong. In opera, for instance, there is a card called "Characterization of Opera," giving in very succinct form the ideal proposed in this form of art. Another general card, "Definition of Qualities in Opera," explains the meaning of the analysis of qualities given in the comparative valuations. This analysis is as complete as it was possible to make after consultation with a large number of the foremost musicians and musical writers of this country. The text is valued as to its musical fitness and its dramatic opportunity; the music as to its spontaneity, elaboration, dramatic truth, and adaptation to the voice; the orchestration as to its beauty of tone color and its dramatic strength. There is yet a farther element of comparison in the scenic demands. The specific cards in this set take up the fourteen great representative operas (allowing only one to each composer). There is a short sketch of the history of the work, and a general estimate of its place in art. Besides, there is a "qualitative analysis," in which the work is marked on a scale of ten in each of the qualities mentioned in the "Definition of Qualities." These valuations are approximate only and must be so understood; nevertheless, they have been made by some of the most competent critics in America, and revised with great care, and finally averaged from the results of many individual valuations made independently. Whatever dissent may be taken from one or the other particular rating, the valuations in the main are just, and afford a new and important assistance to the intelligence in comparing different works with each other, and measuring their approximation to the proper ideal of opera. I may say further, that when the plan of these qualitative valuations was first proposed to musicians, it was rejected unanimously; nevertheless I found by talking with different critics that their estimates of great works were approximately the same or similar, a fact indicating the tacit recognition of certain inherent qualities of the works, and certain standards of valuation. On farther study and consultation I was pleased to find that my idea began to appear practical to these gentlemen, and after some time and many changes we arrived at the definition of qualities and valuations on the cards. If the cards in the opera set be arranged chronologically the student will find that the progress towards complete opera is very manifest, from the recitative of the first opera, Peri's "Eurydice" to the splendid endless melody of Wagner's "Tristan and Isolde." It will be noticed here, and especially in certain departments yet to be considered, that the valuations are high, 10's appearing quite frequently. This is explained by the fact that only masterworks of the different periods and schools find a place here at all.

Class D is devoted to Oratorio. There is one general card, defining the qualities and the ideal of oratorio, and giving also a bird's-eye view of its history. Then follow seven special cards, each devoted to one representative work of this class. Here again the information is given that the student naturally needs. First as to the circumstances of the production of the work, and its period. Then a general estimate of its merit, and reference to its most important musical numbers. In this way are treated the first oratorio, Cavaliere's "Representation of the Soul and the Body," Bach Passion Music, the "Messiah," "Creation," "Mount of Olives," Spohr's "Last Judgment," and "Elijah." In this department the principles of sacred music are contained by implication, and the works chosen are those which mark the highest flights of music in the direction of the sublime.

Class E again takes up the Symphony, the highest type of instrumental music. Here as before there is a general card defining the ideal proper to this form of art, and affording a succinct account of the history of symphony. Then follow seven specific cards each devoted to a particular masterwork, with its history, its qualitative analysis and a general statement of its place as a type, or representative of the class. The composers represented are Mozart, Haydn, Schubert, Beethoven, Mendelssohn Liszt, and Saint-Saens.

Class F. is devoted to the Concerto. There is a general card defining the qualities and the ideal of this form of music, and giving a general idea of the manner in which the concerto had its origin, and the direction of its progsess to the highest point reached. The works chosen are the very greatest. Beethoven's "Emperor," Chopin E minor, Schumann A minor, Mendelssohn G minor, Liszt E flat major, Saint-Saens in G minor, and Paganini in E minor. Each of these comes up for its history, its general points of excellence and superiority, and a qualitative valuation, whereby comparisons are facilitated between different works.

Class G treats of the Sonata in the same manner. Besides the general card defining the qualities of the sonata and giving a general idea of the history of this form of art, seven specific cards follow devoted to C. P. E. Bach's sonata in F, Mozart's sonata in C minor, Haydn's sonata in D, Beethoven's Appassionata, Schubert's sonata in A minor, Weber's sonata in A flat, Schumann's sonata in G minor. These works are compared with each other as to their melodic spontaneity, harmonic strength, thematic development, formal beauty, depth of meaning, fitness for the instrument and pleasing quality. In the cards of this set and the next following, the various writers have been peculiarly fortunate in bringing out the poetic implications of the works discussed, whereby the analysis is elevated out of a mechanical estimate into the realm of pictorial and poetic suggestiveness.

Class H deals with chamber music, the highest type of instrumental music for selected audiences and performers of artistic quality working together in self-forgetfulness towards a mutual end. There is first a general card defining chamber music and its sub-divisions, giving also a short history of this form of art. Then follow seven specific cards devoted to masterworks in this department. They are Grieg's quartet for strings in G minor, Beethoven's string quartet op. 131, Schubert's quartet in D minor ("Death and the Maiden"), Schumann's quintet, Saint-Saen's quintet, and Rubinstein's trio in B flat major, and Brahm's quartet in D minor. These beautiful tone poems, "of finest ray serene," are discussed in a fortunate manner, affording at once a basis of comparative valuation, and a suggestion of their poetical qualities.

Class I is devoted to songs—that form of music so near the daily needs of the amateur, yet so far from discriminating good taste. Here the same plan is followed as in the preceding classes. After the general card defining the ideal of this kind of music, and the qualities which enter into its success, there is a brief historical view of the growth of the song, and the phases of the ideal distinguishing the principal classes from each other. In this department there was such a wealth of material that it was peculiarly difficult to reduce the selections to the number of seven, and still afford a general view of the subject. After many consultations with different experts in this department, the following list was selected as on the whole embodying the best practicable representation within the narrow limits proposed. They are the "Adelaide," of Beethoven, "He the Noblest," of Schumann, the "Erl King," of Schubert, "Palm Trees," by Faure, "Non e Ver," by Tito Mattei, "Home, Sweet Home" and "The Lost Chord," by Sullivan. These, as before, are described, characterized and analyzed for purpose of comparison. It might possibly have been better to have extended the number of selections in this department in order to include representatives of the Franz songs, and the later French and German lieder, but as the number of subjects pressing for recognition was very great in the aggregate, it was thought that the types represented in the selections admitted, practically cover the ground.

The foregoing list, long as it is, embracing six provinces of music, the most important, and no less than fifty-six masterworks in these departments, is far from completing the scope of these studies. Long before the earliest of these masterworks was produced (in 1600), there had been an art of music which prepared the way for these later achievements. There is no illustration of the law of progress more brilliant than that shown in the art of music, if we take it from the earliest appearances of the art, more than 4,000 years before the Christian era, in Egypt, down to the time when masterworks in the modern sense began to be composed. Hence class A is devoted to the antiquities of music, in which music itself is defined and a table of its qualities given upon a general card, with a bird's eye view of its entire history and its great epochs and their relation to each other. Then follow seven specific cards devoted to the representative moments of the ancient art of music, from that of the ancient Egyptians down to the period of Huebald, the first theorist who gives musical examples in musical notation—and consequently the first writer whose music can be understood accurately as to its scale and the order of its melodic make-up. The subjects are: Ancient Egyptian music, of which a running account is given, and a memorandum of their instruments, together with an analysis of qualities (in so far as they can be inferred from the illustrations remaining, several of the most important of which are given in the present volume); ancient Greek music with an account of the classic drama; ancient Hindoo music with an account of the Hindoo drama and the principal instruments of their music; a general card defining early Christian music; St. Ambrose, St. Gregory and Huebald. These celebrated names are placed according to their influence upon the art of music, in the light of the best information attainable, and the characteristic points of their doctrines are given.

After Huebald we enter upon a more advanced period (class B, mediæval music), tending more nearly towards the principles of art now in force. The topics are mediæval secular music, Franco of Cologne and Franco of Paris, with qualitative analyses of their music, Dufay and early polyphony, the great Netherland writers of the next period, Okeghem, Josquin, Willaert and Gombert; Martin Luther and the Protestant chorale, Orlando Lassus and his place in art; Palestrina and pure church music. These two books of sixteen cards contain the gist of the information usually occupying more than a volume in the large musical histories, and the condensation and clearness of the present statements will be highly appreciated by the student, I am quite sure.

Nor have we yet exhausted the information covered by this set of studies. There are still sixteen other general cards, devoted to separate points of general information concerning music, and the less important forms of musical art, such as amateurs often desire, yet find it very difficult to locate. The topics are the principles of musical form, the fantasia, the fugue, the etude, songs without words, the madrigal and its related part songs, the nocturne, the principles of the beautiful, the classical in music, definitions of the romantic, miserere, requiem, te deum, principles of pronunciation of French, German and Italian words, literary interpretation in musical aesthetics, musical history, reasons why it should be studied. Each of these treated analytically and historically, in such a way that the reader is furnished with a synopsis of existing knowledge upon the subject.

If now we review these six great departments of music, represented in the studies, for the purpose of observing the representation made of the greater composers in their different kinds of composition, we find, as would be anticipated, Beethoven at the head, he being represented upon the instrumental side, where his supremacy was greatest, by a symphony, string quartet, concerto and sonata; and upon the vocal side, where he was less great, by an opera, oratorio, and is mentioned upon the mass card and song. Mozart, also, who was one of the universal musicians, is represented by an opera, his requiem, symphony and a chamber quintet. Schubert, again, is represented by symphony, sonata, string quartet and a song. Mendelssohn is represented among the composers of oratorio, symphony, concerto and a general card devoted to the song without words. Weber is represented among the composers of opera and pianoforte sonatas. Schumann is represented on the cards devoted to concertos, sonatas, chamber music, songs, and is especially recognized upon the general card devoted to the romantic. Haydn is represented among the composers of the oratorio, symphony, including especial recognition in the general card as founder of this form, and sonata. Liszt figures in the departments of symphony (symphonic poems), concerto, and is mentioned in the card devoted to the transition from the romantic to the realistic and sensational (see principles of the romantic). Some of the very latest composers are represented here in several departments, as Saint-Saens, who figures as composer of symphonic poems, concertos and chamber music. The total number of composers represented is forty-five, and it is demonstrable that these names include all of those of the very first importance in music, whether we estimate according to beauty of compositions or their historical interest.

I may add that these cards have been written by experts, and represent the latest and most authoritative conclusions upon the several subjects. It should be observed further, that the information here embodied is not common, and much of it cannot be found in encyclopedias, but is the result of original study by the several experts furnishing it.

It will be seen, moreover, that we not only furnish this vast amount of information, in clear and simple form, but, which is much more to the point, *the method, by means of which it can be acquired pleasantly by ordinary students.* This will appear more plainly by reading the directions for conducting the game, especially the "requirements of the progressive grades;" or still better by a carefully conducted trial of it according to the directions. It will then be found that in the earlier exercises the attention is concentrated upon a select part of the entire series, the cards, namely, which concern themselves with vocal music. The general range of this field is acquired by the pupil unconscious to himself, and during the first seven exercises nothing is expected in the way of information beyond the general matters at the top of the cards. With the eighth exercise (or grade) the work begins upon the questions for bringing out the information in the text. With the next grade another class is added, and so on, one point after another being brought out, until at the fortieth exercise the class is supposed to have mastered the information upon the entire ninety-six cards. Those who have done this will be able to comply with the requirements of the higher grades, and will receive a current interest upon their expenditure of study and patience in the way of immediate success in acquiring valuable "books," for precedence in the game. All this will become apparent by noticing carefully the grading requirements and the directions in regard to " acquiring cards." Or by conducting a short trial in any one of the higher grades, permitting (for the sake of the experiment) the players to refer to the text in answering the questions required for gaining cards from other players.

It will also be found that such is the interest and attractiveness of the subject matter, and such its variety, that the present game shows itself far more interesting, and far more varied and fascinating in its practical application, than any game of authors or other similar invention hitherto introduced. This, which the student will eventually discover for himself, has already been so thoroughly demonstrated by the many trials that have been made of the present studies, that the author does not scruple to mention it in this place; since whatever of interest there may be upon the cards is so largely due to the eminent musical gentlemen who have so heartily co-operated with him in preparing them. In this list should be included not only the authors of the specific text upon the cards, identified by initials affixed, and elsewhere given in full (see contents), but also quite a number of others who failed to find leisure for formal contributions, but who have been of important service by suggestions, advice, and occasionally by valuations in special departments. Among these are Signor Eliodoro De Campi, Prof. C. B. Cady, Mr. John S. Van Cleve, Mr. Louis C. Elson, Prof. John C. Fillmore, Mrs. Aubertine Woodward Moore, Mr. Frederick Grant Gleason, the well-known composer and scholar, Mr. A. J. Goodrich, Mr. Emil Liebling, the teacher and pianist, and Mr. W. S. B. Mathews.

Many others were invited to co-operate, but their copy was received too late, or they found it too difficult to condense their ideas into the limits here practicable. But while personally not appearing in cards bearing their initials, many of them were of great service with advice and suggestions, which they were not able to put into writing, owing to a press of professional engagements. Among these Mrs. Sara Hershey-Eddy deserves especial mention.

I feel, moreover, that I ought to make special mention of the aid contributed by the well-known writer, Mr. W. S. B. Mathews, who, besides the cards bearing his signature, has co-operated with me at all stages of the work, and in several cases has been of peculiar service. To all these gentlemen I am obliged for the hearty and efficient quality of their co-operation. The eminence of their names has placed an additional duty upon me to fully complete the plan of the work, and mature the difficult features of it before allowing it to come before the public, to the end that no failure might ensue from some omission of detail. For this reason the studies have taken considerably longer to prepare than was expected, but I feel quite sure that the students will have no reason to regret the delay.

The employment of certain terms, ordinarily associated with games, which make no pretentions to higher purposes than mere amusement, will be regretted by quite a number, as well as by myself. It was inevitable, however, that a game, in which success is measured by the players' aptitude in obtaining and retaining certain groups of cards (representing certain definite parts of the field of knowledge covered by the studies), should avail itself to a certain extent, for greater clearness, of terms, some of which have been designed originally to cover a much less noble kind of triumph.

I will add, further, that I will at any time be pleased to communicate with any who desire to make suggestions or criticisms, or who desire information.

W. M. DERTHICK.

LIST OF SUBJECTS.

Class A. Antiquities of Music.
Definition of Music. Its beginnings.   W. S. B. Mathews. 11
Ancient Egyptian Music.   W. S. B. Mathews. 13
Ancient Hindoo Music.   W. S. B. Mathews. 18
Ancient Greek Music.   W. S. B. Mathews. 20
Early Christian Music,   W. S. B. Mathews. 23
St. Ambrose and early Ecclesiastical Music.   W. S. B. Mathews. 23
St. Gregory and his reforms.   W. S. B. Mathews. 24
Hucbald, Diaphony, Organum and Notation.   W. S. B. Mathews. 24

Class B. Mediæval Music.
Mediæval Secular Music   W. S. B. Mathews. 26
Guido. Solmization and Staff.   W. S. B. Mathews. 26
Franco of Cologne and Franco of Paris. W. S. B. Mathews. 27
Dufay and early Polyphony   L. C. Elson.   28
Okeghem, Des Pres, Willaert and Gombert.   L. C. Elson.   29
Martin Luther and the Protestant Chorale.   W. S. B, Mathews. 30
Orlando Lassus and his place in Art.   L. C. Elson.   30
Palestrina and Pure Church Music.   L. C. Elson.   31

Class C. Opera.
Characterization of Opera.   W. S. B. Mathews. 33
Definition of Qualities in Opera.   W. S. B. Mathews. 33
Eurydice—Peri.   L. C. Elson.   34

Tancredi—Monteverde.	L. C. Elson.	35
Armide—Lulli	A. J. Goodrich.	35
Teodora—Scarlatti.	A. J. Goodrich.	35
Orpheus—Gluck.	F. G. Gleason.	36
Don Giovanni—Mozart.	F. G. Gleason.	37
Fidelio—Beethoven.	A. J. Goodrich.	37
Der Freischuetz—Weber.	W. S. B. Mathews.	38
William Tell—Rossini.	E. de Campi.	38
Huguenots—Meyerbeer.	W. S. B. Mathews.	39
Lucia di Lammermoor—Donizetti.	E. de Campi.	39
Faust—Gunod.	W. S. B. Mathews.	40
Aida—Verdi	A. J. Goodrich.	40
Tristan and Isolde—Wagner.	F. G. Gleason	41

Class D. Oratorio.

Definition of Qualities and Characterization.	W. S. B. Mathews.	42
Representation of Soul and Body—Cavaliere.	J. C. Fillmore.	43
Passion Music—Bach.	J. C. Fillmore,	44
Messiah—Handel.	W. S. B. Mathews.	44
Creation—Haydn.	J. C. Fillmore.	45
Elijah—Mendelssohn.	W. S. B. Mathews.	46
Mount of Olives—Beethoven.	W. S. B. Mathews.	47
Last Judgment—Spohr.	W. S. B. Mathews.	47

Class E. Symphony.

Definition of Qualities and Characterization.	C. B. Cady.	49
Oxford—Haydn.	J. S. Van Cleve.	54
Jupiter—Mozart.	J. C. Fillmore.	50
C Minor—Beethoven.	J. S. Van Cleve.	51
Scotch A Minor—Mendelssohn.	E. Liebling.	51
C Major—Schubert.	J. C. Fillmore.	52
Les Preludes—Liszt.	W. S. B. Mathews.	54
Dance of Death—Saint-Saens.	A. J. Goodrich.	53

Class F. Concerto.

Definition of Qualities and Characterization.	W. S. B. Mathews.	56
E Flat—Beethoven.	W. S. B. Mathews.	57

LIST OF SUBJECTS. xxi

E Minor—Paganini.	W. S, B. Mathews.	62
G Minor—Saint-Saens.		60
E Minor—Chopin.	E. Liebling.	58
G Minor—Mendelssohn.		60
A Minor—Schumann.	E. Liebling.	58
E Flat—Liszt.	E. Liebling.	61

CLASS G. SONATA.

Definition of Qualities and Characterization.	C. B. Cady.	63
E Flat—Haydn.	C. B. Cady.	64
C Minor—Mozart.	J. S. Van Cleve.	65
Appassionata—Beethoven.	J. S. Van Cleve.	66
A Minor—Schubert.	C. B. Cady.	66
G Minor—Schumann.	J. S. Van Cleve.	67
A Flat—Weber.	W. S. B. Mathews.	69
F—C. P. E. Bach.	J. S. Van Cleve.	68

CLASS H. CHAMBER MUSIC.

Definition of Qualities and Characterization,	W. S. B Mathews.	70
Trio B Flat—Rubinstein.	E. Liebling.	70
Quartet for Strings—Brahms.	C. B. Cady.	71
Quartet op. 131—Beethoven.	J. S. Van Cleve.	72
Quartet for Strings—Grieg.	C. B. Cady.	73
Quintet—Saint-Saens.	C. B. Cady.	73
Quartet D Minor—Schubert.	W. S. B. Mathews.	74
Quintet —Schumann.	W. S. B. Mathews.	74

CLASS I. SONG

Definition of Qualities and Characterization.	W. S. B. Mathews.	75
Erl King—Schubert.	W. S. B. Mathews.	76
Home, Sweet Home—Bishop.	W. S. B. Mathews.	76
He the Noblest—Schumann.	W. S. B. Mathews.	77
Lost Chord—Sullivan.	W. S. B. Mathews.	78
Adelaide—Beethoven.	J. C. Fillmore.	78
The Palmtrees—Faure.	W. S. B. Mathews.	79
Non e Ver—Mattei.	W. S. B. Mathews.	77

MISCELLANEOUS.

Fugue.	F. G. Gleason.	88
Fantasie	W. S. B. Mathews.	81
Etude.	W. S. B. Mathews.	81
Nocturne.	J. S. Van Cleve.	82
Madrigal and its related Part Songs.	A. W. Moore.	85
Mass.	W. S. B. Mathews.	91
Requiem.	W. S. B. Mathews.	87
Te Deum.	W. S. B. Mathews.	83
Song Without Words.	J. C. Fillmore.	83
Principles of Pronunciation.	W. M. Derthick.	93
Principles of the Beautiful.	W. S. B. Mathews.	92
The Romantic in Music.	W. S. B. Mathews.	90
The Classical in Music.	W. S. B. Mathews.	86
Literary Interpretation in Musical Æsthetics.	J. S. Van Cleve.	89
Musical History and Reasons Why it Should be Studied.	A. W. Moore.	84
Typical Musical Forms.	W. S. B. Mathews.	80

STUDIES IN MUSICAL HISTORY.

QUESTIONS

CLASS A.—ANTIQUITIES OF MUSIC.

DEFINITION OF MUSIC. ITS BEGINNINGS.

1. What is the meaning of the word Music?
2. Give the technical definition of music.
3. What are the first elements of an artistic music?
4. Give a definition of Rhythm.
5. What is Melody?
6. What is Harmony?
7. What is meant by "innate expression?"
8. What is tone-color?
9. What relation do instruments bear to the foregoing qualities?
10. In what way are the earliest and the latest music related?
11. What have been the actuating forces in the development of music?
12. Which of these came first into operation?
13. What early instance of music does Max Mueller mention?
14. Whence arises the feeling of reverence with which music has been regarded in all ages?
15. What were the earliest hymns used in religious worship?
16. Why are not qualitative valuations assigned to this old music?
17. Describe its musical qualities.

Fig. 1.

Harps, pipe, and flute, from an ancient tomb near the Pyramids.

The group above represented is one of the oldest musical concerts known. It is from a tomb near the great pyramid, and belongs to the IVth or Vth old Egyptian dynasty, dating therefore, approximately, from nearly or quite 4000 B.C. The figures numbered 1 and 3 are playing harps of very antique construction. There is some doubt as to the number of strings upon these instruments, but according to Wilkinson there must have been five or six. From the length of the strings and the structure of the harp the tone must have been in the bass register. The hieroglyph in which the fowl is a prominent feature, designates the figures as "harp scrapers," i. e. players. Figures 2, 4, 5 and 7 are singers, so designated in the inscription above. Figure 6 plays the direct flute, which was a sort of oboe. Figure 8 plays the long traverse flute. Both these are designated as players upon the "pipes." The group is very interesting, and shows that even at that very early period the art of music had attained a development of considerable elaboration.

ANCIENT EGYPTIAN MUSIC.

1. What was the estimation of music among the ancient Egyptians?

2. How has the general character of music in ancient Egypt been ascertained?

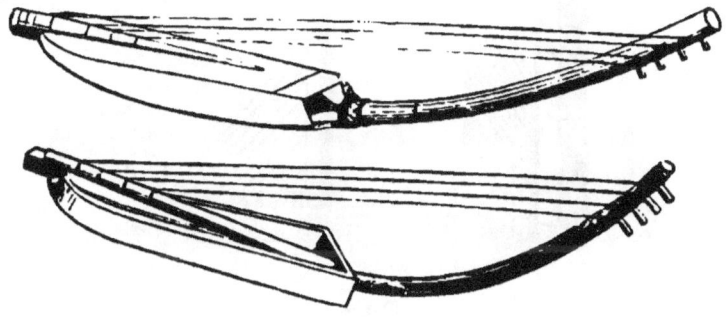

FIG 2.

Fig. 3.

Figure 3 is a group of blind musicians, a harper, a singer and a player upon the banjo, taken from an Egyptian tomb of the middle empire.

3. Where are the oldest tombs, and what is their character and extent?

4. Give the assigned date of the oldest of these representations?

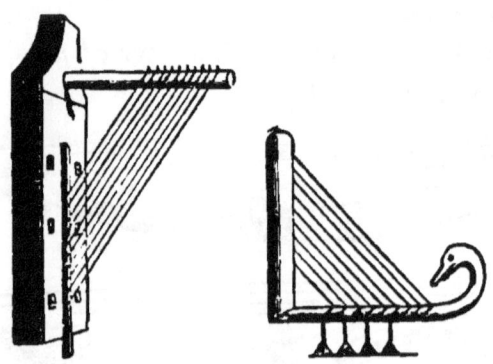

FIG. 4.

5. What were the instruments in these illustrations?
6. How many strings had the harps of that epoch?

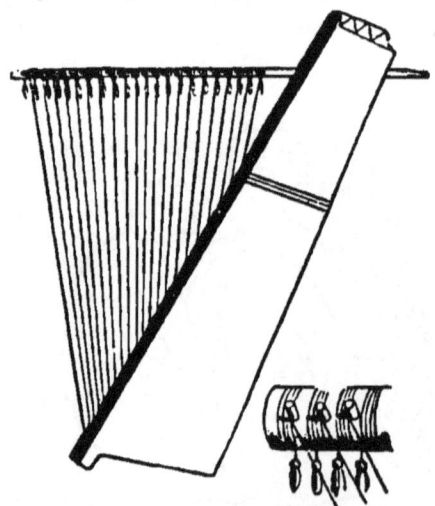

FIG. 5.

Figures 4 and 5 are triangular harps, the kinnor of the Hebrews, the harp which Genesis represents Jubal as inventing, the same which David played before Saul, and the same which the captive children of Israel hung upon the willows of Babylon.

7. In what important structural respect were they unlike our modern instruments? (See Fig. 2.)

8. Describe the harps illustrated in the tomb of Rameses IV. (See Fig. 10.)

9. What change appears in harps of later date?

Fig. 6.

10. What is the largest number of strings mentioned as having been ascertained from the monuments?

11. What other instruments had the Egyptians?

12. Are we to regard the adoption of the Kithara in place of the harp, as an advance in musical appreciation or a step in retrograde?

16   STUDIES IN MUSICAL HISTORY.

FIG. 7.

Figure 6 represents Assyrian harps. Fig. 7, sort of metallic instrument on which the wires or sounding rods were struck by a little metallic mallet or plectrum. The intention of the artist is not very clear. These date from about 2000 B. C.

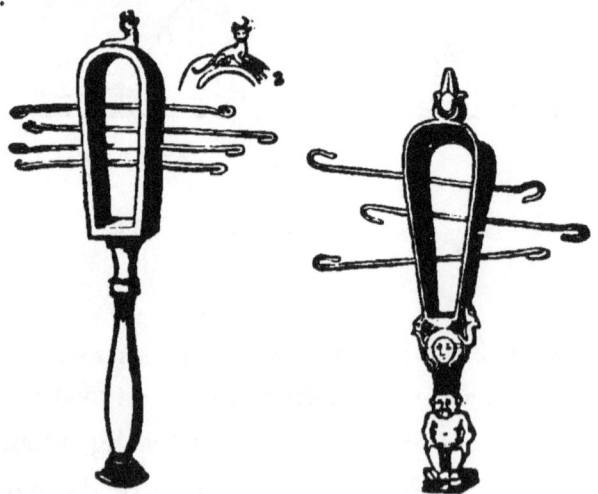

Sistra in the Berlin Museum.

FIG. 8.

Figure 8 consists of sistra, metallic instruments used in Egypt and in the temple service of the Jews, the same as bells now are in the Romish ritual, for notifying the faithful of the most solemn moments of the mass.

STUDIES IN MUSICAL HISTORY. 17

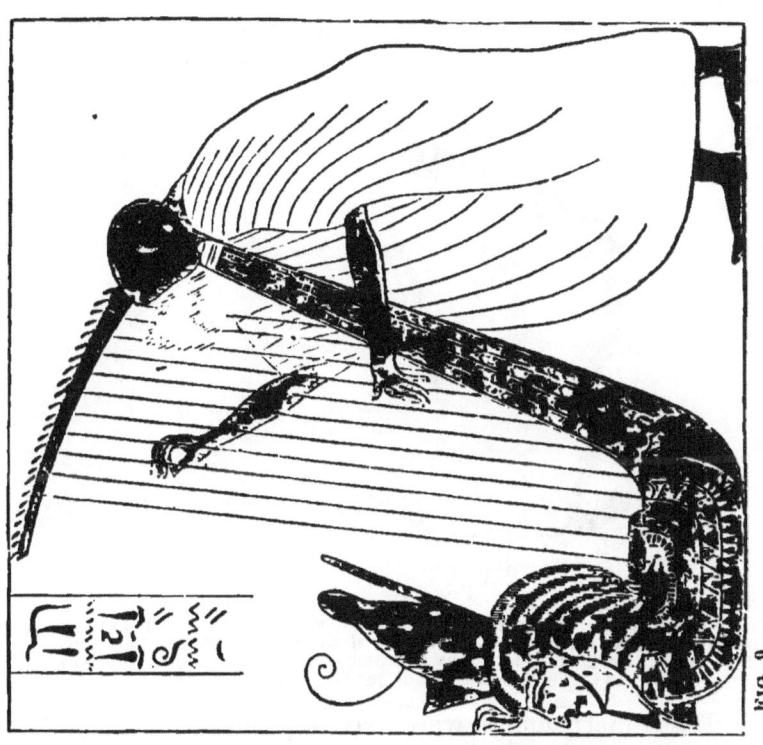

FIG. 9.

Figure 9 is a representation of two harpers, which Bruce, an English traveler, found in the tomb of Rameses IV, about the end of the last century. The players belong to the highest order of the priesthood. The harps are richly ornamented in gold and colors, which, when Bruce first found the paintings, were as fresh as when first put on. The number of strings is eleven on the harp of the left, and thirteen on that upon the right. In the Napoleon description of Egypt the latter is represented with twenty-one strings, which is unwarranted. The date of these instruments was about 1500 to 1600 B. C.

13. How many players are represented as belonging to these ancient orchestras? (See Fig. 1.)

FIG. 10.

Figure 10 is a lyre found in one of the tombs, now in the museum at Leyden. The lyre was a favorite instrument in the time of the later empire. This particular instrument is probably not many centuries older than the Christian era, but the style shows the mode of construction practiced long before.

14. What instruments were used together?

ANCIENT HINDOO MUSIC.

1. What is said of the appreciation of music in India from early times?
2. What especial interest for us has the musical history of India?
3. What is said of the musical value of their instruments of the bow family? (See Fig. 12.)
4. How is it supposed that the idea of the violin came into Europe?
5. What is the characteristic instrument of the Hindoo?
6. Describe the Vina? (See Fig. 11.)
7. How was it played?
8. How many modes had Hindoo musical theory?

FIG. 11.

The Vina is very interesting on account of its great antiquity, which probably reaches back to more than 1000 years B. C. The art of playing it has now been lost. The figure above is a portrait of Jiwan Chah, who lived at Calcutta near the close of the last century, and was the last great master of this instrument. The Vina is the characteristic instrument of India, with which its higher culture of music is associated. It consists of a body of bamboo, with two large gourds for increasing the resonance. It has an elaborate apparatus of frets, part of which are movable, in order to conform to the different scales of India. The six strings were of silk.

9. In what respect was the Hindoo drama like modern opera?

10. At what period was it developed?

11. Into how many intervals did the Hindoo divide the musical octaves?

12. Were their intervals correct? If not, why not?

13. What is said of their discoveries in Harmony?

14. What uses did they make of music?

15. What is said of the players?

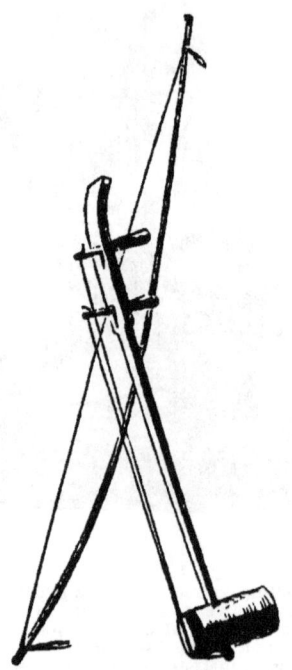

FIG. 12.

The Ravanastron is a rude violin much used in all parts of the east—India, Ceylon, Siam, and by the Buddhist monks in China. It consists of a sycamore box with a parchment top; through this a stick is thrust, and two strings of silk are fastened above and below. It is held for playing in the same position as the modern violoncello. This is probably the very oldest type of all instruments played with a bow.

ANCIENT GREEK MUSIC.

1. What was the earliest music among the Greeks of which we have any account?
2. Of what kind were the songs of the Rhapsodists?
3. What was the Phorminx?
4. How many strings had it?
5. What forms of music came later?

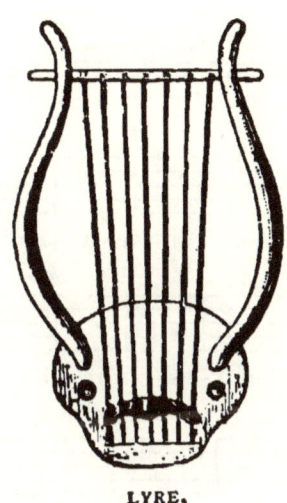
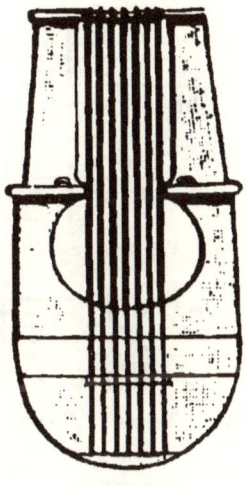

LYRE.   CITHARE.
FIG. 13.

Figure 13 shows the two principal instruments of the Greeks. The lyre, which had the form of a turtle shell with two horns, and the cithara, the improved form of the lyre, which was in use during the period of the Pericles and the building of the Partheon.

6. What was the beginning of Greek musical theory?

7. What consonances did Pythagoras recognize?

8. What important modern consonance is lacking from this list? (The third.)

9. Did you ever hear any music without thirds and sixths?

10. Who was the first real observer of musical phenomena in a musical way?

11. Who was Aristoxenos?

12. What great principle did he enunciate?

13. Who was the last of the Greek musical theorists?

14. What instruments did the Greeks use in their public performances?

15. What was the Aulos?

STUDIES IN MUSICAL HISTORY.

Fragment of first Pythic Ode of Pindar B. C. 490-444. From F. A. Gevaert.

The musical example printed above purports to be a fragment of the music of the first Pythic Ode of Pindar, dating from about 450 B. C. This music was discovered in an old manuscript in Sicily, about two hundred years ago. The musical notation of the Greeks consisted of letters indicating absolute pitch, placed over the syllables to which they applied. As the Greek system was very complicated they had more than 161 characters in their musical notation, all of which had to be remembered arbitrarily. The music of the Greeks was melody without harmony. The movement of this passage was probably quick enough to have a strong and stately effect. Several different interpretations have been given of this ode by various savants. The above is the latest and most authoritative.

EARLY CHRISTIAN MUSIC.

1. What was the course and condition of music after the period described in the study upon ancient Greek music?
2. To what was this decline in musical art due?
3. What influence had christianity upon music?
4. Whence did the early christians derive the music of their songs?
5. What difference is here observed between ancient and modern musical tonality?
6. What cause contributed in this epoch to the modern tendency toward the major tonality?
7. What agency was most active in elevating and developing the art of music for many centuries following this period?

ST. AMBROSE.

1. What circumstance prevented the free cultivation of music during the first four centuries of the christian era?
2. When was christianity formally recognized by the Roman state?
3. How did the adoption of christianity by the Roman authorities affect the art of music?
4. When did St. Ambrose begin to introduce his reforms?
5. What great hymn did he compose?
6. How many modes (scales) did he adopt, and from what were they derived?
7. How long did these scales remain the source of christian music?
8. What characteristic did music acquire through the efforts of St. Ambrose?
9. Mention his principal contributions to liturgical music.

ST. GREGORY.

1. What was the course of music after the death of St. Ambrose?
2. What new reformer arose to correct these abuses?
3. What special service to christianity is accredited to St. Gregory?
4. What was the nature of St. Gregory's reform in music?
5. How many scales were added by St. Gregory, and what were they called?
6. What notes of our scales correspond to the Ambrosian?
7. Give the names of the Ambrosian modes and the notes from which they are reckoned. (See Fig. 00.)
8. Give the names of the Gregorian modes and the notes from which they are reckoned. (See Fig. 00.)
9. In what important respect do these differ from our modern scales?
10. What church tunes have we derived from the Gregorian melodies?

HUCBALD.

1. Who was Hucbald?
2. In what respect was he in advance of other writers upon music?
3. Describe the two forms of musical notation employed by Hucbald.
4. What did the letters "S" and "H S" signify?
5. For what other service is he distinguished in the history of music?
6. Define *Diaphony*.

7. What interval commonly used in modern harmony is omitted in this combination?

8. What effect does this produce upon modern ears, and in what manner is it rendered most noticable?

9. Why does a succession of these chords produce a disagreeable effect, while "each separate chord sounds well enough by itself?"

10. How may we illustrate the peculiar character of this harmony?

11. What was meant by *Organum?*

12. What does it resemble?

13. In what respect does *Organum* differ from *Diaphony?*

CLASS B. MEDIÆVAL MUSIC.
GUIDO.

1. Who was Guido?
2. What was Guido's position at Rome and under whose patronage was he while thus engaged?
3. Wherein consists his importance in musical history?
4. What is meant by *solmisation*?
5. Of what had musical notation consisted for two centuries or there about before Guido's time?
6. From whence are "*neumes*" supposed to have been derived?
7. Describe the general form of these characters.
8. How were "*neumes*" afterward employed?
9. Of how many lines did the staff employed by Guido consist?
10. Of the four lines of the staff employed by Guido, which was green, which red, and for what purpose were they thus distinguished?
11. What other characters than "*neumes*" did Guido sometimes use upon the degrees of his staff?
12. What is here observed of the note-head?
13. How did Guido regard the succession of fifths as taught by Hucbald?
14. What harmonic interval was Guido the first to recognize as a permissible consonance?

MEDIÆVAL SECULAR MUSIC.

1. What are folk-songs?
2. From what source does this class of music spring?
3. What were probably the earliest songs of this character?

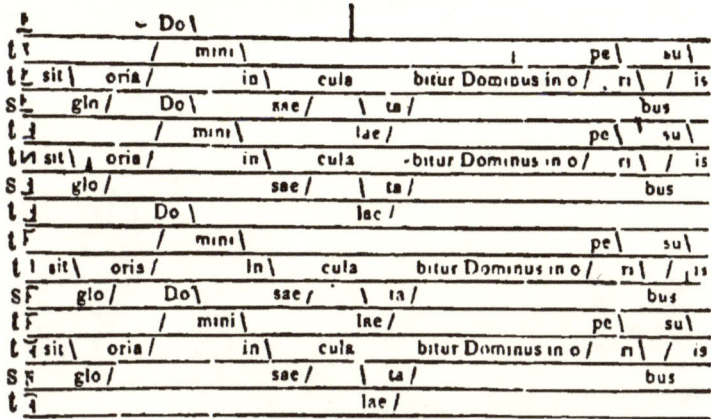

No. 132.—Polyphonic Notation of Hucbald.

Deciphering of above.
Fig. 000.

The above example illustrates the staff proposed by Hucbald, and the manner in which he wrote his famous organum. The syllables are placed in the spaces according to the pitch intended. The initials T and S at the beginning show where the "tones" and "semitones" occur.

4. What conditions promote activity in this department of music?

5. Mention some of the best known songs of this class.

6. What is the difference between the music of the mediaeval epics and the modern popular ballad?

7. Where did the most beautiful melodies of this class have their origin?

8. What class of melodies best illustrate the excellent points in the folk music of the British Isles?

9. In what respect do the folk-songs of England and Germany differ from each other?

10. Why is this class of music peculiarly perishable?

11. What influence has the folk-song exercised upon musical composition?

12. Mention an instance where the works of a great master acquire a peculiar charm from these melodies.

FRANCO.

1. In what respect is Franco of Cologne celebrated in the history of music?

2. What is meant by *mensural* music?

3. About what time were note heads introduced by Franco of Cologne?

4. What was the name given to the note selected as unit?

5. What was its form?

6. How was double the length of this unit note indicated?

7. In what respect did his application of the stem differ from that of the present time?

8. What was the longest note employed by Franco of Cologne called?

9. How was its length indicated?
10. How was the half note indicated?
11. What modifications in these note forms did the Netherland masters introduce soon after Franco?
12. For what were bars first used?
13. What did Franco of Paris contribute to music?
14. Give his classification of the consonances.
15. Give his classification of the dissonances.
16. What new theory did Franco of Paris introduce regarding the use of dissonances?

DUFAY.

1. How many periods are there in the history of the Netherland school?
2. What masters are named as prominent representatives of these four periods?
3. What was the condition of music in the first epoch and what were its characteristics?
4. Who founded the Netherland school?
5. What is stated of Dufay's life and character?
6. In what works are we furnished with a knowledge of Dufay's music?
7. What note character was Dufay the first to employ?
8. What is the character of Dufay's compositions?
9. Of scientific skill and emotional expression which was held in highest estimation at this time?
10. For what number of voices were his works generally written?
11. Did the fugal style exist at this period?

OKEGHEM.

1. Name the principal master of the second epoch of the Netherland school.
2. With whom did he study music?
3. When was he a member of the choir at Antwerp?
4. When did he join the royal choir at the court of France?
5. How long did he remain in the service of the court of France?
6. Name his most talented pupil and greatest successor.
7. What is the style of his works and in what way do they differ from those of his teacher, Dufay?
8. For what number of voices were most of Okeghem's works written?
9. What exception is here instanced?
10. What was Josquin des Pres' rank as a musician?
11. What important appointment did he receive from Pope Sextus IV?
12. How was Josquin regarded by his contemporaries?
13. In what important respect does Josquin's style differ from that of his predecessors?
14. What was the rank of Adrian Willaert?
15. Of what great school was he the founder?
16. What important position did he occupy in Venice?
17. What great musical theorist was among his pupils?
18. With whom did Nicholas Gombert study the art of music?
19. What reason is here assigned for the meager records of the career of Gombert?
20. Of what do his existing works mainly consist.
21. To what position did he finally succeed?

MARTIN LUTHER.

1. Define the principle of individualism?
2. In what department of music was Luther most active?
3. Mention his most celebrated production.
4. What is a chorale?
5. To what kind of hymns were the chorales of Luther set?
6. What is the advantage of retaining a good melody for the service of a particular hymn instead of using it interchangably with any hymn of the same meter as is done in this country?
7. How have these chorales of Luther been treated by later composers?
8. What was Luther's estimation of music?
9. Mention one of Luther's most celebrated hymns.
10. Is the chorale confined to the service of the Protestant church?
11. What is the present condition of the German chorale?

ORLANDO LASSUS.

1. At what age did Lassus give proof of his superior musical abilities?
2. When did he first visit Rome and what appointment did he secure?
3. Where did his career as a composer begin?
4. What objectionable tendency of style peculiar to the earlier masters of the Netherland school did Lassus completely overcome?
5. What is the rank and character of his works?
6. Where and in whose service did he engage after leaving Antwerp?
7. In what esteem was Lassus held by his royal patron?

8. What is the total number of Lassus' works still in existence?

9. What is said of the versatility of his genius in composition?

10. Mention his greatest work.

11. What position does he occupy in relation to the Netherland masters?

12. What two principles was he the first to recognize and employ?

PALESTRINA.

1. At what date is Palestrina known to have been studying music at Rome?

2 To what position was he appointed in 1551?

3. In what respect did Palastrina's fortune differ from that of Lassus'?

4. With whom did he study?

5. Of what important school was he the first and greatest composer?

6. What was his first work and when was it composed?

7. To whom was it dedicated and with what result?

8. For what eminent service is Neri distinguished in the history of musical art?

9. How did Palestrina rank as a composer of church music?

10. For what qualities are his works remarkable?

11. Mention his most important work.

12. What was the condition of church music at the time the Mass of Pope Marcellus was written and what did it demonstrate?

13. How does this work rank with other musical productions of the sixteenth century?

14. What other important works did Palestrina produce?

15. To what class of music did Palestrina almost exclusively devote himself?

16. In what respects does he excell all other ecclesiastical composers?

CLASS C. OPERA.

CHARACTERIZATION OF OPERA.

1. What is the legitimate object of the opera?
2. In what respect does the opera differ from the ordinary drama?
3. What purpose is served by the Recitative?
4. What is expressed in the Arias?
5. What is expressed in the Ensembles and Choruses?
6. Name the three principal elements of the opera?
7. Were the first operas intrinsically valuable or were they merely experimental?
8. Which of the three elements, recitative, aria or chorus, was most prominent in Peri's Eurydice?
9. What three great national schools of opera are here mentioned?
10. What is the most prominent difference between German and Italian opera?
11. Describe the general character of French opera.
12. Describe the writer's ideal of opera.
13. What great composer endeavored to embody all these qualities in his works?

DEFINITION OF QUALITIES OF OPERA.

1. Of what two qualities does a libretto (or opera text) primarily consist?
2. What is meant by "musical fitness?"
3. What is meant by "dramatic opportunity?"
4. What four qualities form the basis of criticism in the vocal music of the opera?

5. What is the importance of "spontaneity" as an element of music?

6. What impression does spontaneity create in the mind of the listener?

7. What is meant by "elaboration?"

8. What is meant by "dramatic fitness?"

9. What is meant by "adaptation to voice?"

10. Of what two elements does the orchestration primarily consist?

11. What is meant by "beauty of tone color?"

12. What is meant by "dramatic strength?"

13. What is meant by "scenic demands?"

EURYDICE, BY PERI.

1. What is said of Peri's parentage?

2. For what is Peri distinguished in the history of music?

3. Under whose patronage was the first opera produced and upon what was it founded?

4. Of what style of music did the origin of the opera mark the beginning?

5. Upon what occasion was Eurydice produced?

6. Who wrote the libretto for this opera?

7. What other name is associated with Peri's in the composition of the music of Eurydice?

8 In what manner was the music chiefly rendered.

9. What accessories were introduced in these early operas?

TANCREDI BY MONTEVERDE.

1. What chords was Monteverde the first to introduce in his music?
2. What school of music was Monteverde the first to supersede?
3. What was the effect upon music of Monteverde's opera "Orfeo?"
4. How many instruments were introduced in the orchestral score to "Orfeo," and of what was this the beginning?
5. What was the importance of the orchestra in "Tancredi?"
6. What important orchestral effects were introduced for the first time in this work?
7. What is Monteverde's rank in the history of opera?

ARMIDE BY LULLI.

1. Of what important school of opera was Lulli the founder?
2. Mention some of Lulli's characteristics as a musical composer.
3. From what was the French opera evolved?
4. What form of overture did Lulli invent?
5. To what kind of effects is the music of Lulli's operas especially adapted?
6. Of what fact relating to Italian opera does Armide afford a striking illustration?
7. To what subjects was the old school of French opera characteristically devoted?

TEODORA BY SCARLATTI.

1. What was Scarlatti's rank as a composer?
2. In what department of music did he most excell?
3. How many operas did Scarlatti compose?

4. What exceptional qualifications did he possess?

5. What was the result of the recent production of some of his works in Italy?

6. In what particulars did Scarlatti surpass his predecessors?

7. What important device, now in common use, was Scarlatti the first to introduce?

ORPHEUS BY GLUCK.

1. In what respect does Orpheus differ from all earlier operas?

2. What actuating idea relative to the opera did Gluck conceive and from what observation was it derived?

3. What did Gluck's ideal contemplate and how did he regard the prevailing style?

4. To what rank did Orpheus assign its composer?

5. What prevailing evil did Gluck successfully oppose?

6. What other great composer has performed similar service for the elevation of the opera?

7. What great composers of instrumental music are here accredited with having contributed to the development of the opera?

8. What prominent excellences does Orpheus possess?

9. In what scene is Gluck's ability as a dramatic writer most forcibly demonstrated?

10. What two qualities of the music are rated highest in the scale of valuation?

DON GIOVANNI BY MOZART.

1. By whom was the libretto of Don Giovanni written, and from what adapted?
2. What is said of the subject upon which Don Giovanni is founded?
3. With what result was the work first presented?
4. How was this opera regarded for some time after its production?
5. What excellences secured for the work such a high degree of favor?
6. What is said of the music of this opera as compared with its dramatic features?
7. How did this work compare in dramatic quality with other works of that period?
8. What two qualities of the music are rated highest in the scale of valuation?

FIDELIO BY BEETHOVEN.

1. What number of operas did Beethoven compose?
2. Upon what was Fidelio founded?
3. Give an outline of the incidents of the plot.
4. Of the musical and dramatic quality of the work, which is most excellent?
5. What probable cause is assigned for the inferiority of this work in comparison with Beethoven's purely musical compositions?
6. To what considerations in the composition of this work did Beethoven evidently give most attention?
7. What two qualities marked highest in the scale of valuation afford evidence of this?

DER FREISCHUETZ BY WEBER.

1. What great distinction has been awarded Weber's Der Freischuetz?
2. What later composer successfully contested the claims of Der Freischuetz to be regarded as the greatest representative German opera?
3. Give an outline of the incidents of the plot?
4. What is the character of the overture to this work?
5. What phase of character peculiarly adapted for dramatic treatment in opera was first introduced in this work?
6. In what other opera of the series here presented is the Mephistopheles character prominently exhibited?
7. What quality in this work, aside from the text, has secured the highest rating in the scale of valuation?

WILLIAM TELL BY ROSSINI.

1. Where was Rossini born and where educated?
2. Mention some of his greatest works.
3. What mark of popular favor did the Parisians bestow upon Rossini on the occasion of the 500th performance of William Tell, and when did this event occur?
4. To what did Rossini devote himself after this period?
5. Where is the action in this opera laid?
6. What are the most notable beauties of this opera?
7. What quality of the music in the scale of valuation is rated highest?
8. What quality of the orchestration is marked lowest?
9. What distinction, when contrasted with Weber's Der Freischuetz, does this suggest between French and German opera?

LUCIA DI LAMMERMOOR BY DONIZETTI.

1. How many operas did Donizetti produce?
2. What characteristic in the effort of composition is Donizetti said to have possessed?
3. How does this opera rank among other works of its author, and what position does it sustain upon the operatic stage?
4. What feature of the work is said to be unsurpassed, and in what does its beauty consist?
5. From what was the libretto of this work adapted?
6. What scene is especially referred to as being highly dramatic?
7. What other features of excellence are mentioned in the text?
8. What two qualities are rated highest in the scale of valuation?
9. In what three particulars, according to the qualitative analysis, is the work most deficient?

THE HUGUENOTS BY MEYERBEER.

1. Upon what historical event is the plot of this opera founded?
2. What celebrated song occurs in the first act?
3. Where is the scene of the second act laid, and what are its prominent features?
4. What is the character of the third act?
5. Where does the fourth act take place?
6. What celebrated piece of music is rendered in the fourth act, and what is its character?
7. What tragic episode occurs in the fourth act?
8. To what is the fifth act devoted?

9. What is said of the score of this work?

10. What quality of the libretto is rated highest in the scale of valuation.

11. What quality of the orchestration is rated lowest.

12. What characteristic of the composer does this indicate.

FAUST BY GOUNOD.

1. How many acts has this opera?
2. With what is the first act concerned?
3. With what does the second act open?
4. What famous song is rendered in the second act?
5. What is the closing feature of the second act?
6. What celebrated scene occurs in the third act?
7. What two great songs are rendered in the third act and by what characters?
8. What is said of the "love music" rendered in the final scene of the third act?
9. What great scene occurs in the fourth act?
10. What two prominent features of this act are mentioned in the text?
11. Where is the final act laid?
12. What pathetic scene occurs in the last act and what is the character of the music?
13. What two features have contributed most to the success of this work?
14. What qualities are rated highest in the scale of valuation?
15. What quality is rated lowest.

AIDA BY VERDI.

1. What four famous operas had Verdi written before he was commissioned to compose Aida?

2. From whom was the commission for this work received?

3. What is said of the magnitude and expense of its production?

4. In what respect is this opera especially unique?

5. What peculiarity of the music is mentioned?

6. In what way has Verdi departed from his former course in the composition of this work?

7. In what respect does this opera correspond to the German ideal?

8. What more recent work of Verdi is said to excel Aida?

9. What valuation has been assigned to the qualities of the Text?

10. What element of the music is rated lowest in the scale of valuation?

11. What qualities of the opera have secured the highest valuation?

TRISTAN AND ISOLDE BY WAGNER.

1. In what respect is Tristan and Isolde the author's most remarkable work?

2. What did Wagner seek to realize in the composition of this opera?

3. How did this work compare with existing models?

4. Characterize the emotional quality of this work in the language of the text.

5. What is said of its musical structure?

6. What is asserted in the opening phrase of the prelude?

7. How is the opera regarded as a whole?

8. How does it rank among the operas presented in this series?

CLASS D. ORATORIO.

DEFINITION OF QUALITIES AND CHARACTERIZATION OF ORATORIO.

1. What is an Oratorio?
2. In what respect does the Oratorio differ from the Opera?
3. From what is the word "Oratorio" derived?
4. To what purpose were the earliest oratorios presented?
5. Who was Emilio Cavaliere?
6. What was the title of his work?
7. In what does its value consist?
8. What was the intrinsic character of the work?
9. From what may its dependence upon the antique ideal be inferred?
10. What was the character of the oratorios which followed this?
11. With what motive were they produced?
12. What prominent characters in the history of music were identified with the second stage of the development of the oratorio?
13. What were Bach's contributions to this form of musical art?
14. What subject was usually selected for presentation by the German masters?
15. In what respect does Handel's Messiah show a divergence from the works of other German masters of that period?
16. Toward what ideal did this divergence tend?
17. What is said of the character of Haydn's Creation as contrasted with those earlier works?

18. What oratorios presented in these studies mark a still further divergence toward the pleasing element?

19. What are the primary qualities of the text of an oratorio?

20. Of what other qualities does the oratorio primarily consist?

REPRESENTATION OF THE SOUL AND THE BODY BY CAVALIERE.

1. In what respect is this work of great historical importance?

2. What other form of musical art had its origin in the same year as Oratorio?

3. What is observed of the points of resemblance and difference between the first oratorio and the first opera?

4. In what respects were they similar?

5. What accessory was employed in this primitive oratorio not admitted in later works of this form?

6. To what subject was the opera originally devoted?

7. Upon what was the oratorio founded.

8. What were the characters of the "moralities" and early oratorios and what did they represent?

9. How were these characters made to progress?

10. What was the play intended to convey?

11. Where were the first performances of the oratorio given?

12. By whom were these early presentations of oratorios given, at what season and with what motive?

13. What two qualities enumerated in the scale of valuation were entirely absent in this work?

14. What valuations are given to "beauty" and "instrumentation" in the scale of qualities?

15. What was the general impression of this work upon the listener?

4. What numbers of the work best represent its characteristic beauties of melody and harmony?

5. Characterize the impression conveyed by this work in contrast with more modern productions, using the language of the text.

6. How does the Creation rank in evidences of technical knowledge and skill?

7. What realistic effects are attempted in the work and how may they be regarded in comparison with modern musical portrature?

8. What quality is rated highest in the scale of valuation?

9. What quality is rated lowest?

10. What is the general impression of the work upon the listener?

ELIJAH BY MENDELSSOHN.

1. Under whose direction was Elijah first produced?

2. What biblical scenes are treated in this work?

3. Give Mendelssohn's conception of the prophet Elijah in his own language as presented in the text.

4. Mention three of the most beautiful solos contained in the work.

5. What is the title of the "angel trio?"

6. Mention the most important choruses.

7. What scene is referred to as being especially dramatic?

8. Describe the scene containing "Holy, holy is God the Lord."

9. What is the general impression produced by this work upon the listener?

CHRIST ON THE MOUNT OF OLIVES BY BEETHOVEN.

1. How many oratorios did Beethoven write?
2. To what period of Beethoven's artistic life does this work belong?
3. What is the musical quality of the work?
4. What was the character of the libretto?
5. How many voices does the libretto introduce and to what characters do they belong?
6. By what character is the first recitative and Aria rendered and what is its title and character?
7. What trio follows the duet between Jesus and the Seraph and what is its character?
8. What number is regarded as the one grand feature of the entire work?
9. How does this chorus compare with other existing works of its class?
10. What other feature of the work is characterized as "beautiful and impressive."
11. What attempts have been made to render the work less objectionable.
12. Which of these attempts is mentioned and in what did it result?
13. What quality is rated lowest in the scale of valuation?
14. What is the general impression of the music upon the listener?

THE LAST JUDGMENT BY SPOHR.

1 How many oratorios did Spohr write upon this theme?
2. When was the first of these produced and with what result?

3. When and from whom did he receive the commission to write the work here treated?

4. What is said of the appropriateness of the title?

5. With what is the oratorio opened?

6. What is the title and character of the first chorus?

7. What two choruses follow the one entitled, "Praise His Awful name?"

8. What descriptive recitative, quartet and chorus, bring the first part to a close?

9. With what does the second part open?

10. What beautiful duet occurs in the second part.

11. What two choruses occur in the second part and what is their character?

12. What is the comparative rank of this oratorio?

13. What class of sacred music does it closely resemble?

14. What is the general impression of this oratorio upon the listener?

15. What qualities of the music are rated lowest in the scale of valuation?

CLASS E. SYMPHONY.

DEFINITION OF QUALITIES AND CHARACTERIZATION OF THE SYMPHONY.

1. What was the term symphony first used to designate?
2. From what class of music was the quartet evolved?
3. Through what means did the symphony attain independence as an instrumental form.
4. With what was its earlier development synchronous?
5. How does the Symphony compare with the Sonata in form and in the conditions of its origin and development?
6. What two classes of pictorial art illustrate the relative importance and character of the Sonata and Symphony?
7. In what way, according to this analogy, does the Symphony excell the Sonata?
8. In what spirit was the Symphony conceived?
9. With whom does the Symphony reach its highest development and purest form? Recite the quotation from Beethoven.
10. What did Haydn contribute toward the development of this form of musical art?
11. What did Beethoven contribute to the Symphony?
12. Who were Beethoven's three greatest successors in the treatment of this form?
13. What composers of the romantic type have excelled in the composition of Symphonies?
14. What is meant by "formal beauty?"
15. What is meant by "originality?"

16. What is meant by "thematic work?"
17. What is meant by "expressiveness?"
18. What is meant by "orchestration?"
19. Upon what does the "pleasing quality" of a work depend?

"JUPITER" SYMPHONY BY MOZART.

1. With what is the form of the symphony identical?
2. In what three works did the form of the symphony culminate?
3. Why is the name "Jupiter" appropriately applied to this work?
4. By whom was the orchestral symphony developed?
5. What works furnished the model for the orchestral symphonies of Haydn?
6. How many symphonies did Haydn compose?
7. In what manner did he spend most of his musical life?
8. What advantages or disadvantages resulted from the limited resources of Haydn's orchestra?
9. What advantages had Mozart over Haydn as a composer of symphonies?
10. In what respects did Mozart surpass Haydn as a result of these advantages?
11. What degree of development was reached in the "Jupiter" symphony?
12. What excellence does the "Jupiter" symphony possess which has never been surpassed even by Beethoven?
13. What other excellences does this work possess in an eminent degree?
14. What two qualities are rated highest in the scale of valuation?

FIFTH SYMPHONY IN C MINOR BY BEETHOVEN.

1. When is it supposed that Beethoven first conceived the ideas contained in this work?
2. What other symphony was finished in the year 1808?
3. What is said of the popularity of the " fifth symphony?"
4. What four notes form the characteristic and impressive motive of this work?
5. In what words did Beethoven express the meaning of these tones?
6. To what does Sir George Grove attribute the greatness of this work?
7. Characterize the work in the language of this eminent writer as quoted in the text.
8. What thoughts are suggested by the first allegro?
9. What is the emotional character of the andante?
10. What impression is conveyed by the scherzo?
11. What is the nature and effect of the finale?
12. Give the final characterization of the work in the language of the text.
13. What does the qualitative analysis indicate?

(*See Manual of Music, page 195.*)

SCOTCH SYMPHONY IN A MINOR BY MENDELSSOHN.

1. From what did Mendelssohn derive the impressions which resulted in the composition of this symphony?
2. What other work resulted from the same experience?
3. What two celebrated overtures had Mendelssohn produced at the age of twenty?
4. Of what peculiar talent did these works give evidence?

5. What is said of the dramatic force of Mendelssohn's works?

6. What is said of the lyric element in his compositions?

7. How does Mendelssohn rank as a master of Form in musical composition?

8. With what does the first movement of this symphony open and close?

9. What is the form of this movement?

10. With what does the second movement open and by what instrument is it rendered?

11. What follows the opening of the second movement?

12. What is said of the character and treatment of the second movement?

13. What is the introduction to the finale?

14. What great English national song is introduced in the finale?

15. What effect has this innovation upon the finale?

16. To whom was this work dedicated?

(See *Manual of Music*, page 355.)

SYMPHONY IN C MAJOR BY SCHUBERT.

1. In what respect was Schubert an exceptional genius?

2. What two characteristics in his works result from this continuous and inexhaustible flow of ideas?

3. In what respect does he materially differ in style from Mendelssohn?

4. Which of Schubert's compositions best illustrates these characteristics?

5. What is the first movement of this symphony?

6. What is the character of the introduction?

7. In what number of measures and by what instruments is the introduction announced?

8. Describe this part of the work in the language of the text.

9. By what instruments is this melody successively taken up and how treated?

10. To what theme does this beautiful melody finally lead?

11. What is the character of the allegro movement?

12. Describe the character of the next three movements in the words of the text.

13. What length of time is required for the performance of this work?

14. How did Schumann regard this symphony?

15. What two qualities are rated highest in the scale of valuation?

DANCE OF DEATH BY SAINT SAENS.

1. What is the character of the scene portrayed in this symphony?

2. To what style or class of music does this work properly belong?

3. What does Saint-Saens say of "program music?"

4. Describe as nearly as possible, without quoting the text, the incidents of the scene suggested by this composition.

5. What two qualities are rated highest in the scale of valuation?

6. In what elements is this symphony inferior as a work of art in comparison with recognized standards?

See Manual of Music, page 500.

LES PRELUDES, BY LISZT.

1. What is the difference of form between a symphonic poem and a regular symphony?
2. In what respect does the ideal of the symphonic poem differ from that of the symphony?
3. Of what style of music was the Les Preludes one of the first compositions?
4. From what did Liszt derive the impressions which characterize this work?
5. Repeat the entire quotation from "Meditations of Lamartine" in the language of the text?
6. Characterize this work in the closing words of the text?
7. What valuation is assigned to the quality of "expressiveness?"
8. What quality is rated lowest and what is the valuation assigned to it?

"OXFORD" SYMPHONY, BY HAYDN.

1. What is Haydn's relation to the development of the symphony?
2. What is the importance of the symphony as a type of instrumental music?
3. When did Haydn produce his first musical composition?
4. When did Haydn produce his last musical work?
5. How many symphonies did Haydn compose?
6. What is Haydn's relation to the development of instrumentation?
7. What meaning for Haydn had the different instruments of the orchestra. (Repeat the quotation given in the text).

8. From what circumstance did the "Oxford" derive its name?

9. How many movements does the work contain and by what are they preceded?

10. What is the general character of the work?

11. What is said of the different movements?

12. What is the general impression of this symphony upon the listener?

13. What characteristic of Haydn is manifest in this work?

14. What is said of the subjects chosen by Haydn for this work and of their treatment?

CLASS F. CONCERTO.

DEFINITION OF QUALITIES AND CHARACTERIZATION OF CONCERTO.

1. What does the term "concerto" imply?
2. What is a concerto?
3. If the intention of the concerto, as stated in the text, be fully carried out, what impression will the listener receive?
4. What consideration has actuated the selection of the concertos presented in these studies?
5. What is the form of the concerto?
6. What is the difference between the concerto and the sonata?
7. From what class of music was the concerto evolved and in response to what desire?
8. By what class of musicians were the earliest concertos written?
9. For what were the earliest virtuoso distinguished aside from their service as executants?
10. What was the result of the efforts of early virtuoso in composition?
11. Why was the result, from a musical standpoint, more favorable under these conditions than under those which exist at the present time?
12. Mention one of the earliest composers in this form.
13. Who was Corelli and when did he flourish?
14. By what successor of Corelli was the concerto brought to greater perfection?
15. What is said of Bach's activity in this department of musical composition? (*See analysis of Bach's Italian Concerto, Manual of Music, page 80.*)

16. What is said of the concertos of Mozart?

17. What is the first condition of a successful concerto according to the text?

18. What is the second condition upon which a concerto depends for its success?

19. What is the third condition of excellence?

20. Which concerto of the present list best exemplifies these principles?

21. What two others come next in rank?

EMPEROR CONCERTO BY BEETHOVEN.

1. How many concertos for piano and orchestra did Beethoven write?

2. When was the first concerto written?

3. What is said of the style of the first of Beethoven's concertos?

4. When was the second concerto written?

5. Give the key and opus number of the second concerto.

6. Give the key, opus number and date of Beethoven's third concerto.

7. Give the key, opus number and date of the fourth concerto

8. What other important works were composed by Beethoven about this time?

9. When was the fifth or emperor concerto written?

10. What important works are mentioned as having preceded this concerto?

11. What is the character of the subject of this work?

12. Who has been most successful in performing this concerto in the United States?

13. What is the general impression of this work upon the listener?

CONCERTO IN A MINOR BY SCHUMANN.

1. For what was the first movement of this concerto intended and when written?
2. When, by whom and under what auspices was the work first rendered in public?
3. What conditions which usually influence the style of less independent writers did Schumann utterly disregard?
4. What does the performance of his works demand of the artist?
5. In what respect are his works inferior to those of Chopin and Mendelssohn?
6. What is said of Schumann's relation to Beethoven?
7. What is the importance of the first bar of the opening theme of this concerto?
8. How is the orchestra treated?
9. What is the meaning of the word *tutti*?
10. What does the first movement include and what is its general character?
11. By what is the closing allegro introduced and what is the technical character of this movement?
12. Mention one reason why this work is not oftener played.
13. What peculiarities render a satisfactory interpretation difficult?
14. What is the general impression of this work upon the appreciative listener?

CONCERTO IN F MINOR BY CHOPIN.

1. How old was Chopin when he produced this work?
2. What other important works had he composed before 1830?

3. What composers are said to have influenced Chopin's style?
4. By what characteristics was Chopin's style distinguished from the beginning?
5. For what instrument was Chopin a favorite composer?
6. What is the character of the orchestral part of this concerto?
7. What is said of Tausig's version of the work?
8. With what does the first allegro open?
9. By what is the bold phrase in the opening of the first allegro followed?
10. How is the second theme introduced?
11. How are the themes treated in this movement and with what does it close?
12. Describe the Romance in E.
13. What is the relative importance of the closing Rondo?
14. What is the treatment of the principal theme and what does it reflect?
15. In what manner are the closing runs of this movement sometimes improperly rendered?
16. How does this concerto compare with the one in F minor?
17. What is said of the second movement of the concerto in F minor?
18. What is the general impression of the present work upon the listener?
19. What two qualities are rated highest in the scale of valuation?
20. What two qualities are rated lowest in the scale of valuation?

CONCERTO IN G MINOR BY SAINT-SAENS.

1. What is Saint-Saens' nationality?
2. How many concertos has Saint-Saens written?
3. Which of Saint-Saens concertos is most popular?
4. What is the style of the opening andante?
5. What follows the opening andante?
6. What is the relative importance of the orchestra in the movement above mentioned and in the Allegro Scherzando?
7. What is said of the popularity of this movement and with what is it compared?
8. To what is the popularity of the Allegro Scherzando attributed?
9. What is here affirmed of the Dance Macabre (Dance of Death) treated in Class E of these Studies?
10. What other prominent master of the French school is here mentioned?
11. What is the last movement of this work?
12. What peculiarity in the last movement is mentioned in the text?
13. What are the technical requirements of the Finale?
14. How is the work regarded by artists and the public?
15. What secures for this work its high rank among concertos?

CONCERTO IN G MINOR BY MENDELSSOHN.

1. What two elements not often united in the works of one composer does this concerto exhibit?
2. What characteristics of classic music are manifest in this concerto?
3. In what is it related to the romantic in music?

4. What is meant by romanticism in music?

5. What does romanticism seek to express and at the sacrifice of what considerations?

6. What moods does the classical ideal imply?

7. In what traits is Mendelssohns relation to the classic and romantic shown?

8. What extreme of emotional expression did Mendelssohn avoid?

9. Mention one of Mendelssohns compositions which most prominently exhibits the romantic spirit.

10. Is this same spirit of romanticism observable in any large number of his works?

11. Of what is this concerto an admirable revelation?

12. What traits of character does it show.

FIRST CONCERTO IN E FLAT MAJOR BY LISZT.

1. Does this concerto differ from former works in this form?

2. To what is this difference attributable?

3. What is the character of the orchestral treatment and with what is it comparable?

4. At what period of the composer's life was this concerto sketched and finished?

5. What other celebrated works were produced in this same period?

6. By whom and on what occasion was it first rendered?

7. In what respect did Liszt deviate at the beginning from the usual form?

8. What does this innovation require of the pianist?

9. Of what is this first part composed and to what does it lead?

10. Describe the movement which follows and leads to the scherzo?
11. What is the character of the scherzo?
12. Describe the movement following the scherzo.
13. With what does the work end?
14. What is the general impression of this work upon the listener?
15. What qualities are rated highest in the scale of valuation?

CONCERTO IN E MINOR, BY PAGANINI.

1. Why is this concerto especially interesting?
2. What is the character of the last movement and what is its relative importance in the work?
3. Of what was Paganini the inventor and what does this work illustrate?
4. What are the "natural harmonics" and how were they employed by Paganini?
5. What technical feats did Paganini introduce in the finale of this concerto?
6. What use of a single string is repeatedly illustrated in this work?
7. What was the apparent object of employing a single 4th or 3rd string where the same tones might have been much more easily obtained from the 2nd or 1st?
8. By what device did Paganini take advantage of the orchestral players who accompanied him?
9. What is the valuation of "display of solo instrument" in the qualitative table?
10. What valuation is given to "concerted effects?"
11. What is the general impression of this concerto upon the listener?

CLASS G. SONATA.

DEFINITION OF QUALITIES AND CHARACTERIZATION OF SONATA.

1. To what does the name sonata apply?
2. During what length of time has the sonata form been in process of development?
3. What does the history of the sonata form reveal?
4. Of what is this form the expressional medium?
5. What two agencies have contributed to the rhythmical element of the sonata?
6. In what respects has the drama contributed to the development of this form?
7. Define the words polythetic and monothetic.
8. In what manner did the people's song contribute to the enrichment of the sonata?
9. In what way has the fugue been an important factor in the development of the sonata?
10. From what primitive word was sonata derived and what was its original meaning?
11. For what purpose was the word sonata first used?
12. What is the present full signification of the word sonata?
13. From what form immediately preceding it in the course of development of instrumental music was the sonata separated or evolved?
14. Of what was the suite composed and in what style was it written?
15. Mention three of the earliest writers of violin sonatas.
16. What composers were among the first to write sonatas for keyed instruments?

17. For what instruments did Sebastian Bach compose in this form?

18. Did these early writers all adhere to a fixed rule or model, or did their works differ, each contributing independently to the formation of the sonata?

19. With what is Haydn accredited in the treatment of this form?

20. What modification in style and treatment do you understand by the substitution of monothetic and fugal for the polythetic idea?

21. What did Beethoven contribute to the sonata form and with what result?

22. What are the primary qualities of the sonata according to the qualitative analysis?

SONATA IN E FLAT BY HAYDN.

1. For what special service is Haydn historically identified with the development of the sonata?

2. Which of Haydn's works were first presented to London audiences?

3. What was Carl Philip Emanuel Bach's service to the sonata form?

4. What is the difference between the fugue and the sonata?

5. By what conditions was the free development of the sonata hindered before this time?

6. What musical element, not before utilized in instrumental composition, did Haydn adopt, which largely determined the melodic and formal character of his works and rendered them so popular?

7. What condition contributed to the freest exercise of Haydn's peculiar artistic pent and rendered his works so original?

8. In what particular is Haydn's study of the folk-song clearly manifest in his music?

9. What other characteristics, not before mentioned, are noticeable in the sonatas of Haydn?

10. In what particulars did he approach nearest to the Beethoven period in his treatment of this form of art?

11. What quality of this work is rated highest in the scale of valuation?

12. What quality is rated lowest?

SONATA IN C MINOR BY MOZART.

1. How does this sonata deserve to be characterized?

2. What is said of the mechanical devices employed in this sonata?

3. What is the style of the opening fantasia?

4. In what keys are the three movements of the sonata proper written and what is said of its form?

5. What is the character of the adagio and what does its treatment exemplify?

6. By what is the orchestra suggested in the opening movement of the fantasia?

7. What rare gift did Mozart possess in a high degree?

8. What is expressed in this sonata?

9. What two chords did Mozart use with remarkable skill?

10. Characterize his treatment of these chords in the language of the text.

11. What quality of this work is rated highest in the scale of valuation?

12. What qualities are rated lowest?

SONATA APPASSIONATA BY BEETHOVEN.

1. What is the comparative importance of this sonata?
2. What does this work represent?
3. What emotions are reflectd in this composition?
4. For what is the first movement distinguished?
5. Of the three thematic elements which is first and of what feeling is it expressive?
6. What is the second theme and what does it suggest?
7. How is the third motive constructed and what does it express?
8. What other work of Beethoven's represented in these studies contains a similarly constructed motive expressive of a like feeling?
9. What is the character of the melody which is placed over against these three thematic clauses?
10. Characterize this movement in the language of the text.
11. What is the andante and how is it treated?
12. Describe the finale.

SONATA IN A MINOR BY SCHUBERT.

1. Describe Schubert's surroundings at the time this sonata was written.
2. Describe the character of Schubert's genius in the language of the text.
3. Characterize Schubert's sonatas in the language of the text.
4. What is said of Beethoven's sonatas and what difference of style does the comparison suggest?
5. What songs did Schubert compose about the time this sonata was written and to what do they furnish a clue?

6. What is the emotional quality of the first movement?
7. What is the second movement?
8. What is said of the third movement?
9. With what does the sonata close and for what is it conspicuous?
10. What quality is rated highest in the scale of valuation?
11. What quality is rated lowest?

SONATA IN G MINOR BY SCHUMANN.

1. What is Schumann's position among composers of instrumental music?
2. Of what does this sonata present an illustration?
3. In what features of this work are Schumann's powers best exemplified?
4. Of what limitations in the art of composition does this work give evidence?
5. How many movements does this work contain and what is the character of the main outlines?
6. What is said of the materials utilized in this work?
7. What departure from the usual custom is observed in the first movement?
8. Of what characteristic of Schumann does the andantino furnish an example?
9. What is the expressional character of the scherzo and rondo and what effect do they produce upon the listener?
10. What is Beethoven's method of building a climax?
11. Characterize the contrary impressions produced

upon the listener by the music of Beethoven and Schumann in the language of the text.

12. What qualities of this work are rated highest in the scale of valuation?

13. What quality is rated lowest.

SONATA IN F MINOR BY C. P. E. BACH.

1. What was C. P. E. Bach's rank among pianoforte virtuosi of his time?

2. What great service to musical art is accredited to C. P. E. Bach?

3. What claim has the present work to special interest and admiration?

4. Of how many movements does the work consist and what are they?

5. What excellences does the work possess and what composers do they suggest?

6. What traces of Sebastian Bach's influence are discoverable in this composition?

7. What qualities of Beethoven does it foreshadow?

8. What is said of the emotional character of this work?

9. What is the character of the rhythms?

10. What is expressed in the melody?

11. What composer and what emotional qualities are mentioned as foreign to the style of this work?

12. What is said of the "chords" and "counterpoint" of the work?

13. What quality is rated highest in the scale of valuation?

14. What qualities are rated lowest?

SONATA IN A FLAT, BY WEBER.

1. Of what school of musical art in its full development was Weber the first great representative?
2. How many sonatas did Weber write?
3. What other great composer produced some of the best of his works in this form at the same time?
4. What is said of the form of this sonata?
5. What is the character of the first movement?
6. What is said of the second movement of the sonata?
7. How is the theme of the second movement afterward treated?
8. What is the character of the menuetto?
9. What is the finale?
10. How does this work rank in point of difficulty?
11. What was Weber's rank as a pianist at the time this sonata was written?
12. Characterize the work in the language of the quotation from Ambros.

CLASS II. CHAMBER MUSIC.

DEFINITION OF QUALITIES AND CHARACTERIZATION OF CHAMBER MUSIC.

1. What does the term "chamber music" imply?
2. For what class of players is chamber music written?
3. What is the difference between chamber music and concerto music?
4. Why does the performance of chamber music require players of eminent and equal ability?
5. In what sense is a chamber piece more than a concerto?
6. What names are applied to chamber pieces and why?
7. When is the term "string" added or prefixed?
8. What is the relative importance of the piano when used with other instruments in a piece of chamber music?
9. Who perfected the form of the string quartette?
10. What other composers excelled in the composition of works in this form?
11. Why is it difficult to give a satisfactory definition of qualities applicable to all the specimens of chamber music selected for these Studies?
12. What qualities should an ideal chamber piece contain?

TRIO IN B FLAT MAJOR BY RUBINSTEIN.

1. To what school or class of composers does Rubinstein belong and what is his rank?
2. In which does Rubinstein most excel, composing or piano playing?

3. In what respect does Rubinstein's music differ from that of other writers of the new Russian school?
4. What composers are most prominent in the Russian school at the present time?
5. In the treatment of what forms has Rubinstein been most successful?
6. What symphony of exceptional merit has Rubinstein composed?
7. What is the character of the present Trio?
8. What special merits are mentioned in the text?
9. What mood is reflected in the adagio?
10. By what is the adagio contrasted and with what effect?
11. For what is the finale written and what is its relative merit?
12. What criticism may be inferred from the closing sentence of the text?
13. What quality is rated highest in the scale of valuation?

QUARTET IN C MINOR BY BRAHMS.

1. Who was "the mighty Cantor of Leipsig" with whom Brahms is here compared?
2. What intellectual powers does he possess in common with Sebastian Bach?
3. What other qualities essential to a great composer does he possess?
4. On what plane of study is the real power of the present work most deeply felt?
5. In what respects are Bach, Beethoven and Brahms related in musical art?

6. What broader scope and significance is ascribed to the music of these three composers?

7. How must we listen to this quartet if we would understand it?

8. Is this quartet to be regarded as a classic or as a romantic composition?

9. Characterize this composition in the words quoted in the last four lines of the text.

10. What quality is marked highest in the scale of valuation?

STRING QUARTET, OP. 131, BY BEETHOVEN.

1. What is the importance of the string quartet as a form of instrumental music?

2. What masters have written perfect works in this form?

3. What other quartets of Beethoven rank equally high in merit with this one?

4. What impression do Beethoven's later works produce upon the superficial listener?

5. How do they appear to the profound scholar?

6. What change came over Beethoven toward the end of his life, and how did it affect his compositions?

7. What emotions are embodied in this quartet, and what in its entirety does it represent?

8. What point in musical development does this work attain?

9. Recite the closing phrase of the text.

10. What is remarkable in the valuations assigned to the qualities of this work?

G MINOR QUARTET BY GRIEG.

1. Of what race is Edward Grieg a descendant?
2. Where was Grieg educated?
3. What was the source of his musical inspiration?
4. What national characteristics are reflected in his compositions, and in what manner?
5. What was the character of Grieg's remote ancestors?
6. How is the spirit of this ancient race revealed in the music of Grieg?
7. What essential element of the classic does this quartet lack?
8. What is expressed in this composition, and in what does its unity consist?
9. What is the characteristic quality of Grieg's larger works, and to what school do they belong?
10. What quality is rated highest in the scale of valuation?

QUINTET FOR PIANO AND STRINGS, BY ST. SAENS.

1. To what nation does Saint-Saens belong by birth and education?
2. What characteristics of his music ally him to the French school?
3. In what characteristics is he related to the German school?
4. What is said of the character and importance of this quintet?
5. For what is this quintet especially remarkable?
6. What characteristic of all his chamber music is plainly illustrated in this composition?
7. To what especial points of interest and merit in this work does the writer refer?

8. Quote *verbatim* the closing sentence of the text?
9. What quality is rated highest in the scale of valuation?

QUARTET IN D MINOR, BY SCHUBERT.

1. Upon what poem and song was this quartet founded?
2. What does the poem represent?
3. What is the character of the music in the song?
4. What two great instrumental works were written about the time of this quartet?
5. How many subjects has the first movement and what does each suggest?
6. From what is the second movement developed and what is its character.
7. In what respect is this work especially interesting?
8. What quality is rated highest in the scale of valuation?

QUINTET IN E FLAT, BY SCHUMANN.

1. What is the rank of this quintet among other chamber pieces by Schumann?
2. Upon what occasion was it produced and by whom was the pianoforte part rendered?
3. What composer carried its fame to Paris?
4. Describe the first movement of the work.
5. What is the second movement designated and how treated?
6. What is said of the finale?
7. What characteristics of Schumann's music are well illustrated in this work?
8. What has secured for this work its great popularity?
9. What quality is rated highest in the scale of valuation?
10. What quality is rated lowest?

CLASS I. SONG.

DEFINITION OF QUALITIES AND CHARACTERIZATION OF SONG.

1. What is meant by song?
2. What is the character and importance of this class of music?
3. What does the term song technically imply?
4. What originally was the fixed type of verse for song?
5. What is said of the structure of song melodies at the present time?
6. What is said of the present style of our song literature?
7. What is the character of the most popular songs? Give examples.
8. How are these simple songs commonly designated?
9. To what does the term "ballad" properly apply?
10. What was the first modification of the simple ballad which tended toward the development of a more elaborate song form?
11. What is the most elaborate song form extant?
12. What is its character? Give examples.
13. What term is applied to the simplest songs of the French, and what is their character?
14. What other large class of song literature do the Germans possess?
15. What is the character of these short songs, and what composers have been active in their production?
16. Define the Aria.
17. What is the character of the English ballad?
18. What must be the character of a song text?

19. What three essential qualities of the music in its relation to the text are mentioned?

20. To what other requirements than those of the text must the music of the song lend itself?

21. What is the relation of the pianoforte to the song?

ERL KING, BY SCHUBERT.

1. What was the Erl King in German and Scandinavian mythology?

2. What is the story as represented in Gœthe's ballad?

3. What is said of the origin of this song?

4. Whence the special importance of the Erl King as a type of song?

5. What two qualities are rated lowest in the scale of valuation?

HOME, SWEET HOME, BY BISHOP.

1. In what representation does this song surpass all others in the estimation of English speaking people?

2. By whom was the poem written and what was his condition in life?

3. What is said of the origin of the music?

4. What distinction is mentioned between the Scottish and English folk songs and those of the Germans.

5. In what respect do songs of this class differ from the Italian?

6. What is the merit of songs like Home, Sweet Home from an æsthetic standpoint?

7. What quality is rated highest in the scale of valuation?

8. What valuation is assigned to "harmony" and "accompaniment?"

HE THE NOBLEST, BY SCHUMANN.

1. What is said of the relation between Schubert and Schumann as song writers?
2. In what respect does Schumann surpass Schubert?
3. What is said of the voice and instrument as related to the text of the song?
4. What practice common among song writers (especially Italian) did Schumann disregard?
5. What is said of the songs, 'Woman's Love and Life?''
6. What is the character of the present song?
7. What qualities are rated highest in the scale of valuation?

NON E VER, BY MATTEI.

1. Of what is the present song illustrative?
2. What is said of the melody of this song?
3. To what does this work owe its effect upon the hearer?
4. What is the relative importance of music and text in songs of this character?
5. What is said in evidence of the popularity of this song?
6. Characterize the spirit of the music by quoting the stanza given in the text?
7. Define the character of the melody and its treatment?
8. What quality is rated highest in the scale of valuation?
9. What quality is marked lowest in the scale of valuation?
10. With what school of song do these valuations suggest a wide distinction?

LOST CHORD, BY SULLIVAN.

1. In what particular does the Lost Chord rank among the best?
2. Quote the lines of the poem given, and repeat the paraphrase of the writer.
3. What is said of the relation of the music to the words?
4. What is said of the melody, harmony and accompaniment of this song?
5. What "clever points" in the music are mentioned and where do they occur?
6. What is the character of the music at the climax?
7. What is the relation of this work to the Italian Romanza and the German song?
8. What distinction is here mentioned between the Italian Romanza and the German song?

ADELAIDE, BY BEETHOVEN.

1. What is said of the "nature" of Beethoven?
2. What emotional characteristics distinguish Beethoven's greatest works?
3. What attitude of mind with reference to the Divine is manifest in Beethoven's compositions?
4. What is the emotional character of Adelaide?
5. What is revealed in the music of this song?
6. In what respects is Adelaide different from most other love songs?
7. What is the character of the first movement of the song?
8. Describe the second movement.
9. What elements have received the highest valuation in the qualitative analysis?
10. What is the valuation of the text?

PALM BRANCHES, BY FAURE.

1. Of what national school of song is "Palm Branches" a type?
2. Describe the Chanson.
3. What is the character of the "song proper," as created by Gounod, Faure and other French writers?
4. What combination of qualities render these songs so effective for the concert room and church?
5. Why are they sometimes objectionable for the latter purpose?
6. Upon what is Faure's Palm Branches founded, and what is its rank among songs of its kind?
7. What is the character of the melody and accompaniment in this work?
8. To what is the peculiar strength of the melody of this song attributable?
9. Describe the manner in which this effect is secured.
10. What quality is rated highest in the scale of valuation?

MISCELLANEOUS.

TYPICAL MUSICAL FORMS.

1. Define the term "form" in its application to music?
2. What is the most important principle of form and in what way is it manifested in music?
3. What is the order of dependency between the period, the motive and the phrase?
4. What is said of the order and manner of this repitition?
5. Symmetry has reference to what?
6. What is the relation of contrast to form?
7. When may art be said to enter into form?
8. From what roots have all musical forms been derived?
9. What has the last named kind of musical structure been called and what have grown out of it?
10. What has the former—the lyric people's song—produced?
11. Into what complex forms do these two radical types unite and in what manner?
12. Of what is Fugue the type?
13. Of what is the Song Without Words the type?
14. In what respect does the Nocturne differ from the Song Without Words?
15. Of what is the Fantasia the type?
16. What is said of the Sonata in comparison with other musical forms?
17. What is a "character" piece?
18. What vocal forms are mentioned as important?

FANTASIE.

1. Define the term fantasie.
2. What does the German term "phantasie' signify?
3. Define "fantasie" in its application to music:
4. What is the meaning of "potpourri?"
5. Since when has the word fantasie been in use and what was its meaning in music?
6. What is the character of Bach's Fantasies?
7. To what form did the fantasie approximate during the Beethoven period?
8. For what purpose was it sometimes applied to sonatas?
9. What composers have written fantasies with but little variation from the sonata form?
10. What is the character of many pieces of Schumann's to which this term is applied?
11. What do the fantasies of one generation prophesy of the next following?
12. What objectionable tendency results from a too close adherence to the style of accepted models?
13. How does this ultimately effect music and in what way is freedom of style again restored?
14. What masters have created the greatest works of this name?
15. For what does the fantasie stand?
16. When does the fantasie exceed its proper limit?

QUALITIES OF ETUDES.

1. What is the meaning of the word "Etude?"
2. What is the object of mechanical studies?
3. Mention instances of higher kinds of studies.

4. Mention certain studies equally interesting as music and exercises?
5. What is said of Schumann's compositions?
6. What is their value for practice?
7. What studies are at the other extreme in the scale of value?
8. Why are the etudes of Czerny, Koehler, Schmitt and others of their class less useful than exercises which pretend to no musical value?
9. Where do the studies of Loeschhorn, Cramer, Gurlitt and Reinecke belong in the scale of merit?

NOCTURNE.

1. From what was the word Nocturne derived?
2. What is a nocturne?
3. What is said of the form of the nocturne?
4. What is the usual character of the melodies of which the nocturne is composed?
5. What class of emotions find expression in the nocturne?
6. Who was the inventor of the nocturne?
7. What is the general character of the Field nocturnes?
8. In what respects do Chopin's nocturnes surpass those of Field?
9. Characterize the four Chopin nocturnes mentioned in the words of the text?
10. What picture is represented in the last part of the text? (Note: When desirable, students may be required to quote this in the language of the text.)

SONG WITHOUT WORDS.

1. To whom do we owe the suggestive title Songs Without Words?
2. Are the Songs Without Words of Mendelssohn to be regarded as classical or romantic compositions?
3. To what school of musical art does Mendelssohn really belong, the classic or romantic?
4. What is the distinctive mark of the classical school?
5. What is the characteristic mark of the romantic school?
6. Give the views of the romanticist in the language of the text.
7. To what school was Mendelssohn allied by nature and education?
8. What is said of Mendelssohn's treatment of form?
9. Towards what style of art did Mendelssohn's feelings incline him?
10. What did he seek to express in his Songs Without Words?
11. Why is the title which Mendelssohn applied to these pieces so appropriate?
12. In what sense are these compositions romantic?
13. In what sense are they classic?
14. What influence have the charming compositions and the title applied to them exercised upon musical art?

TE DEUM.

1. Who composed the original music of the "Te Deum?"
2. What is said of this Ambrosian melody?
3. When and in what manner was it introduced into England?

4. What early composers used the Ambrosian melody as the basis of their settings of this text.

5. Among the later settings of the Te Deum, which are most celebrated?

6. Who was first to employ orchestral accompaniment in his setting of this hymn?

7. What is said of Purcell's Te Deum?

8. What is said of Handel's "Utecht" Te Deum?

9. Describe Berlioz's Te Deum.

10. What is the character of more recent settings of this hymn!

THE HISTORY OF MUSIC. REASONS WHY IT SHOULD BE STUDIED.

1. How can we correctly estimate the creations of the human mind?

2. Why has music been called the most subjective of all arts?

3. Why is a knowledge of the origin and growth of tone forms indispensable?

4. To what does the study of the history of music form a reliable guide, and why?

5. What does it teach us about the birth and growth of music?

6. What does it show about the folk-song and later music?

7. What do we learn from it about notation, harmony and melody?

8. What do we learn from it about instrumental music?

9. Besides instruction what does it afford?

10. What is a musical education without it?

11. Why is it peculiarly advantageous to the musician?

THE MADRIGAL.

1. Give the etymology of the word madrigal.
2. To what was the term madrigal first applied?
3. What was the character of the songs of a later period bearing this title?
4. What was the source of the music and poetry of the madrigal?
5. To what is due its development as a distinct musical form?
6. What school of musical art contributed most to its development and what prominent master is mentioned?
7. In its earlier phases what form of vocal art did the madrigal resemble?
8. What was the character of the Motet?
9. What was the course of the development of the madrigal and in what did it culminate?
10. Who perfected the form of the madrigal and transplanted it in Italy?
11. What prominent Italian master composed in this form?
12. When was the madrigal introduced into England?
13. What conditions rendered England so favorable to the development of the madrigal at that time?
14. What English composers contributed to this form and with what result?
15. What related part songs are mentioned?
16. What is a Round?
17. What is the distinction between the Round and the Catch?
18. Of what vocal form peculiar to England were these the immediate precursors and when did it originate?

THE CLASSICAL IN MUSIC.

1. From what source was the word "classic" derived, and what its original and present meaning?
2. What tests must a work of art undergo before it may be declared a classic?
3. To what must a work be adapted to attain the rank of a classic?
4. What are the elements of classic merit?
5. What is "style" in art?
6. What is "truth" in art?
7. Why may each generation have its own standard of classic excellence, rejecting those of former periods?
8. To what class are the best of earlier works consigned when superseded by those of a more advanced period?
9. What productions mark the beginning and close of the Classical Period in music?
10. What school of musical art followed the Classical?
11. What works produced between 1600 and 1827 may properly be regarded as classic?
12. What elements of merit must the compositions of earlier periods possess to retain a place among modern works?
13. What composers have produced the best classical works?
14. What æsthetic elements do the best of the works contain in equal proportion?
15. What has Hegel, the great esthetician predicated as the measure of the classic?
16. To what class of music does the term classical properly belong?
17. What are the forms of the classic in music?

18. Which of these forms did Beethoven develop to the highest degree of classic beauty and excellence?

19. What misuse of the term classic is referred to in the text?

REQUIEM.

1. To what is the name "Requiem" applied?
2. From what is its name derived and what is its English translation?
3. By what is this anthem followed?
4. To what music are these pieces assigned?
5. What is said of these old melodies?
6. What is the first important setting referred to in the text?
7. What movements did Palestrina's setting contain?
8. Why is it supposed Palestrina omitted from his setting the remaining three movements?
9. What is said of Mozart's Requiem. (See Manual of Music, revised edition, page 146.)
10. What is said of Cherubini?
11. Describe Brahm's "German Requiem."
12. What is said of Berlioz's setting of this text?
13. What is said of Verdi's Requiem?
14. What part of the text affords the best opportunity for effective musical treatment?
15. In what respect do modern composers differ from the old masters in their treatment of this text?

THE FUGUE.

1. What is the rank and character of the fugue as a form of musical art?

2. From what was the fugue derived?

3. What element does it possess not contained in the canon?

4. How many voices are required to give expression to the fugal form?

5. What is the first requisite of the fugue?

6. What must be the theme or subject?

7. How is the subject announced and how treated?

8. What are these successive representations called collectively and what is their relative importance in the composition?

9. In what key does the first voice sing the subject?

10. How is the subject treated by the responding voice and what is it there called?

11. What is the melodic material furnished by the voice, while the "answer" or repitition is being sung by the second voice called?

12. Must this melody, which follows the subject, always be the same or may it be varied at each repetition of the subject?

13. What subjects are permitted to sing, either the subject or the answer in course of the exposition?

14. What is the chief feature of the exposition?

15. What appears at the close of the exposition?

16. How is the "interlude" treated and of what materials is it composed?

17. How does the interlude close and what then appears?

18. How are the exposition and interlude relatively treated during the continuance of the piece?

19. In what key must the last exposition appear?

20. How is the last exposition treated when the nature of the subject permits?

21. What is meant by *Stretto?*

22. May these repetitions be appropriately used before the final exposition?

23. Is it preferable to introduce such combinations during the progress of the piece or reserve them for the last?

24. What is sometimes added at the close?

LITERARY INTERPRETATION IN MUSICAL ÆSTHETICS.

1. What phase of musical art did the eighteenth century originate and bring to perfection?

2. What phase did the nineteenth century develop?

3. What composers are mentioned as the supreme types of the "Classical" in music?

4. What composers are distinguished for the "realism" of their music?

5. What three composers are here assigned the highest rank and in what province of musical art did each excel?

6. What is "programme music?"

7. What is the character and value of the literature which has attended the development of programme music?

8. To what extent may these "literary spurs" be useful?

9. What extreme is to be avoided in the acceptance of these literary paraphrases?

10. In what composer do the musical tendencies of the eighteenth and nineteenth centuries unite?

11. What work of Mendelssohn's is referred to as being too obviously realistic to require mention?

12. What is suggested by the initial motive of six notes in Mendelssohn's overture to the Hebrides?

13. Under what circumstances was this work written?

14. Finally, what is the value of these "literary aids" to musical interpretation?

DEFINITION OF THE "ROMANTIC."

1 What in general is meant by the term romantic and to what is it commonly applied?

2. What is the meaning of romantic in its application to music?

3. When did the romantic spirit begin to be prominent in music and of what was it a part?

4. Name the first distinctly romantic composition and give the date of its publication?

5. What earlier instances are mentioned in which "picture painting" was attempted in music.

6. Who was the first of great romantic writers; when and in which of his works is the romantic spirit most prominent?

7. What composer followed Schubert and for what instrument were his works mostly written.

8. What work of Mendelssohn marks a great advance in musical representation?

9. What has been the character in this respect of most works written since Schumann and Mendelssohn?

10. What is the character of some of Liszt's com-

positions in comparison with those of other composers of the romantic school?

11. What modern composers mentioned have conformed to the classic model?

12. What are the characteristic forms of romantic music?

13. Why is the Song Without Words necessarily romantic?

14. Why is the Fantasie a characteristic form of the romantic?

15. What is sensationalism in music?

16. What is realism in music?

THE MASS.

1. What is meant by "Mass?"

2. How many texts are included in the Mass and how are they frequently treated?

3. Mention the first text referred to and the names included in it.

4. Mention the second text and all it includes.

5. Mention the third text and what it includes.

6. Mention the fourth and fifth texts with all they include

7. What is often added to the parts named and where does this addition occur?

8. What is said of the original music of the Mass?

9. When was the Ambrosian and Gregorian music supplanted and what then formed the *cantus fermus?*

10. What was still later taken as foundation for the music of the Mass and what example of this style is mentioned?

11. What is said of Palestrina's "Missa Papæ Marcelli?"

12. When and by whom, after Palestrina, was the next great work of this class written?

13. In what respects does Bach's Mass in B minor differ from Palestrina's "Missa Papæ Marcelli?"

14. What is said of Mozart's Masses?

15. After Bach's great work what was the next important contribution to this department of music?

16. What is said of Beethoven's "Missa Solemnis?"

17. What more recent settings are mentioned and what is their character?

THE PRINCIPLES OF THE BEAUTIFUL.

1. To what sense does every work of art first appeal, and with what general result?

2. Upon what does a work of art first depend for its popularity, and power to reach the mind?

3. Beyond the mere sensuous impressions produced by a work of art, what other pleasurable manifestation does it afford?

4. In what particular is this skill or power of execution revealed in painting?

5. What manifestations of skill in music produce pleasureable impressions?

6. What kind of pleasure does the evidence of skill afford, and what does it require of the observer?

7. What other impressions than those referred to is a work of musical art capable of producing?

8. Do all observers experience an equal degree of emotional effect from a work of art?

9. What class of observers does a work of art appeal to most strongly?

10. Upon what is the realization of the deepest emotional effects of art dependent?

11. What is the range of emotional feeling afforded by a musical work?

12. According to this classification, what is the first and lowest degree of pleasure derivable from art?

13. After the "pleasing in sensation," what is the next higher plane of aesthetic enjoyment?

14. What is the third and highest degree of pleasure afforded by art, and what is its range?

15. May all music be classified in accordance with these principles?

16. What masters have written the most spiritual of all music?

KEY TO PRONUNCIATION.

1. Give the Italian sound of a.
2. What two sounds has the Italian e?
3. Give the Italian sound of i.
4. What two sounds has the letter j in Italian
5. Give the two sounds of the Italian o.
6. What is the Italian sound of u?
7. What sound has the vowel a in German?
8. What is the sound of ai in German?
9. What sounds has ae or ä in German?
10. What sound has aeu or aü in German?
11. What sound has au in German?
12. What sounds has e in German?
13. What sound has ei in German?
14. What sound has eu in German?

15. What sound has i in German?
16. What sound has ie in German?
17. What sounds has o in German?
18. What sound has oe or ö in German?
19. What sound has u in German?
20. What sound has ue or ü in German?
21. What sounds has a in French?
22. What sound has ai in French?
23. What sounds has au in French?
24. What sounds has e in French?
25. What sound has ei in French?
26. What sound has eu in French?
27. What sounds has i in French?
28. What sound has ia in French?
29. What sounds has ie in French?
30. What sounds has o in French?
31. What sound has u in French and how indicated?
32. Explain the use of y in French?

QUESTIONS FOR A NORMAL COURSE OF TWELVE LESSONS.

DEFINITION OF MUSIC.—CLASS A, ANTIQUITIES OF MUSIC.

1. What is the meaning and what the derivation of the word music?
2. What are the elements of a perfect music?
3. What have been the actuating forces of musical progress?
4. How do you account for the reverence in which the art of music has been held by the Aryan race in all ages?

ANCIENT EGYPTIAN MUSIC.

1. What is the source of our knowledge concerning the music of the ancient Egyptians?
2. What were the instruments most in use?
3. What evidences of progress are mentioned?
4. What are the more usual combinations of players for band purposes?

ANCIENT HINDOO MUSIC.

1. Wherein consists the importance of the history of Hindoo music?
2. Describe the course through which the primeval instrument of the violin family came into Europe.
3. What was the characteristic instrument of Hindoo music?
4. What is said of their theory, and of the state of the art of music among them?

ANCIENT GREEK MUSIC.

1. Describe the general course of music among the ancient Greeks.

2. Who were the principal composers of the classical drama, and what modern form of art did it resemble?

3. Who were the principal musical theorists among the Greeks?

4. Who were the first observers of musical phenomena by ear among the Greek writers?

EARLY CHRISTIAN MUSIC.

1. What is supposed to have been the character of the music of the early Christians?

2. Wherein was christianity important in the development of the art of music?

3. How did christianity operate in elevating the art of music?

4. What is said of the connection of christianity and music from its beginning until now?

ST. AMBROS.

1. What was the character of the singing of the early christians?

2. What cause is mentioned as having first contributed to a larger official recognition of music?

3. What is said of the poetical and musical gifts of St. Ambros?

4. What was the nature of his musical reform upon its technical side; and what upon the spiritual?

ST. GREGORY, THE GREAT.

1. What became of St. Ambros' reform after his death?

2. Who arose next to uphold the standard of pure church music?

3. What was the nature of St. Gregory's addition to the musical theory of St. Ambros?

3. Describe the scales introduced by St. Ambros and Gregory, and tell which of our modern church tunes have been derived from them.

HUCBALD.

1. Who was Hucbald, and wherein is he interesting in musical history?
2. Describe his notation, and state what he meant by the letters H and S.
3. What was Diaphony?
4. What was Organum?

CLASS B, ANTIQUITIES OF MUSIC. MEDIÆVAL MUSIC.

1. Who was Guido of Arezzo?
2. Describe the Neumes and the progress towards notes and a staff.
3. What was the musical notation of Guido?
4. What progress does Guido mark in the direction of harmonic discrimination?

FRANCO OF COLOGNE AND FRANCO OF PARIS.

1. What is the ground of the celebrity of Franco of Cologne?
2. Describe his notation.
3. With what department of music is the name of Franco of Paris associated?
4. What classifications did he introduce in harmony?

DUFAY AND EARLY POLYPHONY.

1. Who were the leading masters of the four great epochs of the musical history of the Netherlands?
2. Give the personal history of Dufay.

3. What are the contrapuntal features of his compositions that have come down to us?

4. What is the limitation of his music upon the æsthetic side?

OKEGHEM, DES PRES, WILLAERT AND GOMBERT.

1. Who was Okeghem, and what the style of his music?

2. Who was Josquin dés Prés, and what is said of his music?

3. Who was Willaert, and what the nature of his musical work?

4. What is said of Nicolas Gombert?

MARTIN LUTHER AND THE PROTESTANT CHORALE.

1. In what sense might Luther be taken as a forerunner of the romantic?

2. How did Luther become influential in the musical development of Germany?

3. What is a chorale, and will you mention a celebrated specimen composed by Luther?

4. What is said of the influence of the chorale beyond the bounds of the Protestant church and in later times?

MEDIÆVAL SECULAR MUSIC.
(GENERAL CARD OF THIS CLASS.)

1. What is meant by Folks Song?

2. What is said of the older Folks Song?

3. What of the Folks Song in later times?

4. Why have we so few examples of the older Folks Song, and where in modern music can we trace their influence?

ORLANDO LASSUS.

1. What objectionable tendency of style peculiar to the earlier masters of the Netherland school did Lassus completely overcome?
2. What is the rank and character of his works?
3. What position does he occupy in relation to the Netherland masters?
4. What two principles was he the first to recognize and employ?

PALESTRINA.

1. Of what important school was Palestrina the first and greatest composer?
2. How did Palestrina rank as a composer of church music?
3. For what qualities are his works remarkable?
4. What was the condition of church music at the time the Mass of Pope Marcellus was written, and what did it demonstrate?

CLASS C. OPERA.

CHARACTERIZATION OF OPERA.

1. Define and characterize the Opera.
2. What purpose is served by Recitative, Aria and Chorus respectively?
3. Describe the prominent differences between French, German and Italian Opera.
4. Describe the writer's ideal of opera.

DEFINITION OF QUALITIES OF OPERA.

1. State and define the qualities of the opera text.
2. State and define the qualities of the music of the opera.
3. State and define the qualities of the orchestration of opera.
4. What is meant by scenic demands?

EURYDICE, BY PERI

1. What is Peri's chief claim to distinction among musical composers?
2. What names are mentioned in connection with Peri's in this study, and what is the relation of each to the events described?
3. What is the musical character of this work?
4. What is said of the stage accessories in these early operas?

TANCREDI, BY MONTEVERDE.

1. For what is Monteverde most celebrated in musical annals?
2. Describe the character and influence of his "Orfeo."

3. What is the character and importance of "Tancredi?"

4. To what position is Monteverde assigned in the history of music?

ARMEDE, BY LULLI.

1. What is Lulli's position as a composer of operas?
2. What were Lulli's chief characteristics?
3. From what was French opera evolved?
4. What is said of his operas in general, and of Armede in particular?

TEODORA, BY SCARLATTI.

1. What is said of Scarlatti's rank and fecundity as a musical composer?
2. What were Scarlatti's qualifications, and what is said of the revival of his works?
3. What did Scarlatti contribute to the improvement of the opera?
4. What is said of many of his librettos and the present importance of his works?

ORPHEUS, BY GLUCK.

1. In what respects does this opera differ from all earlier and contemporary works?
2. What did Gluck's ideal contemplate, and from what observations were his ideas derived?
3. What is Gluck's position among opera writers of his time, and what was the nature of his reform?
4. What is the character of this work?

DON GIOVANNI, BY MOZART.

What is said of the libretto and subject of this opera?

2. To what beauties of this work is its popularity chiefly due?

3. Of the dramatic and musical features of the work which are most prominent?

4. How may we account for the disparity between the musical and dramatic features of the work?

FIDELIO, BY BEETHOVEN.

1. How many operas did Beethoven compose, and upon what is the present work founded?

2. Describe the plot of the opera.

3. What is observed of the musical and dramatic quality of this work?

4. How may we account for the fact that the music is superior to the dramatic features of the opera?

DER FREISCHUETZ, BY WEBER.

1. What is the relative importance of this work among operas?

2. What is the story of the opera?

3. Give a general description of the incidents of the plot.

4. What is said of the orchestration, and what phase of character was first presented in this opera?

WILLIAM TELL, BY ROSSINI.

1. Where was Rossini born, and where educated, and what are his principal operas?

2. Where is the action of the present work laid?

3. What strong national characterization is mentioned in the text?

4. What are the most notable beauties of this opera?

THE HUGUENOTS, BY MEYERBEER.

1. Upon what is the plot of this opera founded?

2. Describe the first act of the opera.

3. Describe the fourth act.

4. What is said of the score of the opera?

LUCIA DI LAMMERMOOR, BY DONIZETTI.

1. How many operas did Donizetti compose, and what is said of his characteristics as a musical writer?
2. What is the rank and character of this opera?
3. What is said of the challenge scene?
4. Give other interesting particulars of the opera.

FAUST, BY GOUNOD.

1. Describe the first and second acts of the opera.
2. Describe the third act.
3. Describe the fourth and fifth acts.
4. Upon what does the opera rest for its success?

AIDA, BY VERDI.

1. Mention four of Verdi's most important operas.
2. Upon what was the text of Aida founded, and what were the circumstances of its first production?
3. What characteristics of the work are mentioned?
4. What is the implied difference between this and the composer's earlier works?

TRISTAN AND ISOLDE, BY WAGNER.

1. What is the general character of this work, and what did the composer seek to realize in its production?
2. What is the emotional character of the work?
3. What is said of its musical structure?
4. What is said of the opening phrase?

CLASS D. ORATORIO.

DEFINITION OF QUALITIES AND CHARACTERIZATION OF ORATORIO.

1. Define Oratorio and state from what source the name was derived.

2. What was the character and importance of Cavaliere's Representation of the Soul and the Body?

3. By what was Cavaliere's work followed, what composers were active in the second period of oratorio, and what was the subject of their works?

4. Mention the primary qualities of Oratorio?

REPRESENTATION OF SOUL AND BODY, BY CAVALIERE.

1. What were the points of resemblance and contrast between the earliest oratorios and the earliest operas?

2. Upon what was the oratorio founded, and what were the characters represented?

3. What three characters were represented in this oratorio, and how were they treated?

4. What was the object of this oratorio, and what were the circumstances of its production?

PASSION MUSIC, BY BACH.

1. What is the character and importance of this oratorio?

2. To what is the scripture text largely set, and to what characters assigned?

3. What is expressed in the chorus, and with what is the text interspersed?

4. Give a further description of the work.

MESSIAH, BY HANDEL.

1. What is the rank and character of this oratorio?
2. Describe the first part, mentioning the vocal numbers which it contains.
3. Describe the second part, giving its vocal numbers.
4. Describe the last part, and give a further characterization of the work.

CREATION, BY HAYDN.

1. What is the most striking characteristic of Haydn's Creation?
2. What are the principal choruses, and what is said of their character?
3. What distinction is implied between this and many of the most celebrated works of the present?
4. What is said of the technical knowledge and skill and the dramatic quality displayed in this oratorio?

MOUNT OF OLIVES, BY BEETHOVEN.

1. What is said of the quality of the libretto and the style of the music in this work?
2. What solo voices are introduced, and what are the principal numbers mentioned?
3. What special point of merit does the work contain?
4. Give further interesting particulars of the work.

ELIJAH, BY MENDELSSOHN.

1. On what occasion, and under whose direction, was this work first produced?
2. What are the scenes treated in this oratorio?
3. What are the most beautiful solos in the work?
4. What are the greatest choruses, and what thrilling effect is described?

LAST JUDGMENT, BY SPOHR.

1. What numbers are introduced in the first part of this work, and what is their character?

2. With what does the second part open?

3. Mention the principal numbers introduced in the second part.

4. What is the character of the music of this composition?

CLASS E. SYMPHONY.

DEFINITION OF QUALITIES AND CHARACTERIZATION OF SYMPHONY.

1. Describe the conditions of the origin and development of the Symphony.
2. Define the form of the Symphony, and state in what respects it differs from the Sonata.
3. With whom did the symphony attain its purest form, and what composers represent the romantic type?
4. Define the qualities of symphony.

"OXFORD," BY HAYDN.

1. What did Haydn do for the sonata form?
2. What did he contribute to instrumentation?
3. Describe briefly the various movements of the work.
4. What is the general character of this symphony, and what peculiarities of Haydn's music does it illustrate?

JUPITER, BY MOZART.

1. What is Mozart's relation to the development of musical form?
2. What advantages had Mozart as a composer of instrumental music which Haydn had not?
3. What stage in the development of the symphony form does the present work represent?
4. In what particulars does this work rank with the best?

FIFTH IN C MINOR, BY BEETHOVEN.

1. How long is Beethoven supposed to have been engaged upon this work?
2. What is the leading motive of this symphony and how was it characterized by Beethoven?
3. What peculiarities of the work are referred to by Sir George Grove?
4. Characterize the different movements of the work in the language of the text.

SCOTCH A MINOR, BY MENDELSSOHN.

1. From what is Mendelssohn supposed to have derived the impressions which characterize this work?
2. What characteristics of Mendelssohn are referred to in the text?
3. Describe the second movement of the work.
4. Describe the adagio and finale.

C MINOR, BY SCHUBERT.

1. What characteristics of Schubert are mentioned in the text?
2. Describe the introduction to the first movement of the present work?
3. How is the opening melody afterward treated?
4. What is the character of the allegro and of the three remaining movements?

LES PRELUDES, BY LISZT.

1. In what respect does the symphonic poem differ from the regular symphony?

2. What inspired Liszt to the composition of this work?
3. Characterize the work in the language of Lamartine.
4. How has Liszt realized these "incidents of the soul?"

DANCE OF DEATH, BY SAINT-SAENS.

1. What is said of the scene described in this work?
2. Describe the scene portrayed to the introduction of the "dance motive."
3. Describe the scene following the introduction of the "dance motive."
4. What has Saint-Saens said concerning "programme music?"

CLASS F. CONCERTO.

DEFINITION OF QUALITIES AND CHARACTERIZATION OF CONCERTO.

1. What is a Concerto?
2. What is the form of the Concerto?
3. From what class of music was the Concerto derived and by whom were the earliest concertos written?
4. Upon what does the excellence of a concerto depend.

EMPEROR E FLAT, BY BEETHOVEN.

1. How many concertos did Beethoven write, and what is the character of the first?
2. What work immediately preceded the Concerto in E Flat?
3. What is the character of the present work?
4. Mention other interesting particulars concerning this concerto.

E MINOR, BY PAGANINI.

1. Why is the present work especially interesting?
2. What is meant by "natural harmonies?"
3. What was the object of using a single string for "long scales and arpeggios?"
4. What questionable advantage did Paganini take of the players who accompanied him?

G MINOR, BY SAINT-SAENS.

1. Describe the opening movement of this work.
2. With what work is the present concerto compared, and in what respects are they similar?
3. Describe the last movement.
4. What is said of the popularity of the work as a whole?

E MINOR, BY CHOPIN.

1. What is said of Chopin's style?
2. Describe the first movement of the present work.
3. Describe the Romance.
4. Describe the closing Rondo, and mention other interesting particulars concerning the work.

G MINOR, BY MENDELSSOHN.

1. What characteristics of Mendelssohn does this work illustrate?
2. What is said of Romanticism in this study?
3. What is said of the Classical in this study?
4. Of what is the present work a revelation?

A MINOR, BY SCHUMAN.

1. For what was the first movement originally intended and what was the occasion of the earliest performance of this work?
2. What is stated of Schumann and his works generally?
3. Give a general description of this concerto.
4. What is said of the difficulties attending the performance of the work?

E FLAT MAJOR, BY LISZT.

1. To what facts is the originality of the present work attributed and what is the character of the orchestral treatment?
2. To what period of the composer's life does the present work belong?
3. Describe that part of the work which precedes the Scherzo.

Describe the Scherzo and add other interesting particulars of the work?

CLASS G. SONATA.

DEFINITION OF QUALITIES AND CHARACTERIZATION OF SONATA

1. Characterize the Sonata as a form of art.
2. What were the sources of its development and what did it derive from each?
3. What was the original and what is the present signification of the word "sonata?"
4. Mention the names of those who have been prominently identified with the history of this form.

F MINOR, BY C. P. E. BACH.

1. What is C. P. E. Bach's relation to the history of the Sonata?
2. What is the general character of the present work?
3. Of what two great composers is the style of this work suggestive, and what characteristics of each does it reflect?
4. What is said of the emotional quality of the work?

E FLAT, BY HAYDN.

1. What is Haydn's relation to the history of the Sonata?
2. What service is attributed to C. P. E. Bach in this study?
3. What final step did Haydn accomplish which contributed materially to musical development and rendered his works so popular?
4. What other characteristics of Haydn's are referred to in this study?

C MINOR, BY MOZART.

1. What is the rank and character of the present work?
2. Describe the opening Fantasie.
3. Of how many movements is the Sonata proper composed, and what is said of the Adagio?
4. What is said of the opening Fantasie, and of Mozart's use of the Tonic Triad and the Dominant Seventh?

APPASSIONATA, BY BEETHOVEN.

1. What is the rank and emotional character of this Sonata?
2. Describe the first movement.
3. What is said of the lyric element in the key of A Flat?
4. Describe the andante and finale.

A FLAT, BY WEBER.

1. What important position does Weber sustain with reference to the Classical and Romantic schools of music?
2. What is the general character of this work?
3 Describe the three movements referred to in the text.
4. Characterize the work by quoting the language of Ambros.

A MINOR, BY SCHUBERT.

1. Describe the surroundings amid which this work was written.
2. What is the character of Schubert's genius as a composer?
3. What is the character of his sonatas?
4. Describe this sonata.

G MINOR, BY SCHUMANN.

1. What is Schumann's rank in musical art, and what characteristics are referred to in the text?

2. What is the character of the present work and what innovation does it represent?

3. What is said of the three movements mentioned in the text?

4. What points of contrast between the works of Schumann and Beethoven are referred to in the text?

CLASS H. CHAMBER MUSIC.

DEFINITION OF QUALITIES AND CHARACTERIZATION OF CHAMBER MUSIC.

1. What does the term chamber music naturally imply and for what class of players is it written?

2. Wherein does chamber music differ from concerto music?

3. What names are applied to chamber pieces and what is the importance of the piano when employed?

4. What composers have produced the most beautiful chamber music and what is said of each?

E FLAT QUARTET, BY BEETHOVEN.

1. What is the importance of the string quartet, what composers are mentioned and what is said of them?

2. What is meant by Beethoven's "third period," and what is said of his later works?

3. What mental habits mark the closing years of Beethoven's life and how did they affect his manner of composing?

4. Describe the present work?

QUARTET IN D MINOR, BY SCHUBERT.

1. Describe the poem and song upon which this quartet is founded.

2. Describe the first movement of the work.

3. Describe the second movement and state what follows.

4. In what particular is the work especially interesting?

QUARTET IN E FLAT, BY SCHUMANN.

1. What is the rank of this quartet; when and under what auspices was it first produced?
2. Describe the first movement of the work.
3. Describe the second movement, the scherzo and the finale.
4. What characteristics of Schumann are illustrated in this work?

TRIO B FLAT MAJOR, BY RUBINSTEIN.

1. What in general is said of Rubinstein and his characteristics as a composer?
2. Give a general description of the present work.
3. What is said of the adagio, the scherzo and the finale?
4. What defects are mentioned in the text and with what qualifications?

QUARTET IN C MINOR, BY BRAHMS.

1. In what respect does Brahm's style resemble Bach's and Beethoven's
2. What is the character of the present work and upon what plane must we seek for its real power?
3. Characterize the music of Bach, Beethoven and Brahms?
4. Characterize this work in the language of the quotation contained in the text.

QUINTET, BY SAINT-SAENS.

1. In what respects is Saint-Saens related to the French and German schools?

2. What is the rank of this quintet and for what is it remarkable?

3. What special beauties are refered to in the text?

4. What is said of its relation to the classic and romantic?

G MINOR QUARTET, BY GRIEG.

1. What is said of Griegs' ancestry and education?

2. What characteristic does he possess in common with Chopin?

3. What does his music suggest or reveal?

4. Describe the present work and state wherein Grieg is allied to the romantic school.

CLASS I. SONG.

DEFINITION OF QUALITIES AND CHARACTERIZATION OF SONG.

1. What is meant by song and what does the term imply?
2. What is a ballad and what class of songs does the term imply? Give examples
3. Describe the German song and the French "Chanson."
4. What is an Aria?

ADELAIDE, BY BEETHOVEN.

1. What is said in this study of Beethoven's nature?
2. How does the present work illustrate these characteristics?
3. Describe the first movement of the song
4. Describe the second movement.

ERL KING, BY SCHUBERT.

1. What is the Erl King in Scandinavian and German mythology?
2. Describe the poem and the song.
3. Mention the circumstances attending the production of the Erl King.
4. What other important facts are given in the text?

NON E VER, BY MATTEI.

1. Of what class of songs is Non e Ver an illustration and what is the character of the melody?
2. To what is its effect chiefly due.
3. What is said of this class of songs?
4. Give a general description of this work.

HE, THE NOBLEST, BY SCHUMANN.

1. In what respects did Schumann surpass Schubert in the composition of the poetic and descriptive song?
2. What is the importance of the pianoforte in Schumann's songs?
3. What did Schumann seek to express in his songs, and what considerations did he disregard to attain this end?
4. To what event in Schumann's life is this song related, and what is its character?

PALM BRANCHES, BY FAURE.

1. Describe the two principal types of French song.
2. What qualities render songs like this effective for the concert room, and why are they less appropriate for the church?
3. Describe Palm Branches.
4. In what respect is the melody of this work one of the most remarkable?

HOME, SWEET HOME, BY BISHOP.

1. What does this song most truly represent?
2. What do we know of the history of the song?
3. What differences between the English and Scotish folk-songs and the German folk-songs are referred to in the text?
4. How do songs like this differ from the Italian, and what is their rank from an æsthetic standpoint?

LOST CHORD, BY SULLIVAN.

1. In what respects does this song rank with the best?
2. By whom was the poem Lost Chord written, and what imaginary incident does it describe?
3. What is said of the music of the song?
4. Between what two classes of songs does this work stand, and why?

MISCELLANEOUS.

THE CLASSICAL IN MUSIC.

1. Define the term Classic, and state the conditions upon which a musical work may be so designated.
2. Name and define the elements of classic merit.
3. Who were the prominent classical composers, and what is said of the best of their works?
4. What are the forms of the classic, and what misuse of the term is mentioned?

LITERARY INTERPRETATION.

1. What is said in this study of the eighteenth and nineteenth centuries, and what composers represent the extreme tendencies in music during this time?
2. What is "programme music?"
3. Under what limitations may literary aids to musical interpretation be helpful?
4. What eminent composer has written works of unmistakable realism; what are they, and what do they suggest?

THE HISTORY OF MUSIC.

1. How may we correctly estimate the creations of the human mind, and why is music its most perfect mirror?
2. To what is the study of musical history a reliable guide, and what does it teach?

3. Besides the instruction afforded by the study of the history of music, what other benefits does it confer?

4. Why is a musical education imperfect without a knowledge of musical history?

TYPICAL MUSICAL FORMS.

1. What is meant by "form" in music?
2. Define the principle of Unity in musical form.
3. Define Symmetry and Contrast.
4. From what two roots are all musical forms derived? Describe them.

FUGUE.

1. Define the Fugue.
2. Define the "Subject," "Exposition," "Answer" and "Counter Subject" of the fugue.
3. Define the "Interlude" of the fugue.
4. Explain the limitations and usages governing the last exposition.

FANTASIA.

1. Give the general definition of the term fantasy and explain the meaning of "Fantasia" in its application to music.
2. What was the original use of the term fantasia and what has been its signification in later periods.
3. What relation has the fantasia in one generation to the generation next following.
4. What variety of works may be classed under this term and what are its limitations?

QUALITIES OF ETUDES.

1. What is the meaning of the word Etude and what class of musical compositions is included under this term?

2. Mention works which are of equal value from a musical and from a mechanical standpoint.

3. What class of etudes occupies the lowest place in the scale of value? Mention composers.

4. What other class of etudes is mentioned? Name representative composers.

NOCTURNE.

1. Give the derivation and explain the character of the composition designated by the word Nocturne.

2. Who invented the nocturne and what is the character of his works in this form?

3. Who surpassed Field in this department of musical composition and wherein did he excel?

4. Characterize some of the nocturnes of Chopin.

THE MADRIGAL.

1. Explain the signification of the word Madrigal.

2. Give an account of the origin and early history of the madrigal.

3. What Netherland and Italian composers produced works in this form and when was it introduced into England?

4. Mention some of its related Part-songs and describe them.

THE MASS.

1. What is meant by "Mass?"

2. Give the names of the texts and sub-texts of the mass.

3. What is said of the origin and early history of the music of the mass?
4. What composers have written the greatest works in this form and what are they?

REQUIEM.

1. Describe the Requiem.
2. Give title and description of Palestrina's great Requiem
3. What is said of Mozart's Requiem?
4. What other important works in this form are mentioned?

TE DEUM.

1. Give the origin, character and early history of the Te Deum.
2. Describe Purcell's Te Deum.
3. What is said of Handel's "Utrecht" Te Deum?
4. Describe Berlioz's Te Deum.

SONG WITHOUT WORDS.

1. State the points of distinction between the Classical and Romantic schools, as defined in this study.
2. What was Mendelssohn's position in musical art with reference to these two schools?
3. What did Mendelssohn seek to express in his Songs Without Words, and are they classical or are they romantic?
4. What influence have these works exercised upon later compositions?

KEY TO PRONUNCIATION.

1. Give the sounds of the Italian vowels.
2. Give sounds of the separate vowels in German.
3. When two vowels occur together in the same syllable in a German word, which should be sounded?
4. Give sounds of the separate vowels in French.

THE PRINCIPLES OF THE BEAUTIFUL.

1. To what does a work of art first appeal, what impressions is it capable of producing, and upon what does it depend for its claim to popularity?
2. Beyond the agreeable impressions of seeing or hearing, what other kind of pleasure does a work of art afford?
3. What is the highest pleasure derivable from art?
4. Explain the three planes of æsthetic pleasure afforded by art.

DEFINITION OF THE ROMANTIC.

1. Define Romantic in its general sense, and also in its application to music
2. When did the romantic spirit begin to be prominent in music, and what was the first distinctly romantic composition?
3. What three great masters of the Romantic school followed Von Weber, and what is said of their music?
4. What are the characteristic forms of the romantic, and what is meant by "sensationalism" and "realism" in music?

INSTRUCTIONS.

SECTION I. CLASSIFICATION OF THE CARDS.

There are three kinds of cards in the Studies, which follow slightly different rules for acquisition and combining.

1. SPECIFIC CARDS, bearing a class letter, "A," "B," "C," etc., each one devoted to some particular composer, work, or period. With four exceptions all specific cards bear qualitative analyses of the subjects to which they are devoted. The exceptions are in Class A, "Early Christian Music;" and in Class B, "Martin Luther," "Okeghem," and "Palestrina." The qualitative valuations were omitted from these in order to gain space for important historical matter, and also because the state of music in the period to which they refer is shown on other cards of the same period. These cards are treated in the game precisely the same as the other specific cards, excepting that it is not possible to augment the valuation of books by agreement among them. (See Sec. III). Specific cards combine with others of the same class, with general cards of the same class, or with unclassified general cards.

2. CLASSIFIED GENERAL CARDS, bearing class letters "A," "B," "C," "D," etc., and without qualitative

analyses. These combine only with specific cards of the same class or with unclassified general cards. The general card of Class A is "Definition of Music," and in Class B "Mediaeval Secular Music."

3. UNCLASSIFIED GENERAL CARDS, not bearing the class letters at the top. These combine with each other or with cards of either of the two other classes.

SECTION II. HOW BOOKS ARE COMPOSED.

1. Two specific cards of the same class and two general cards, which must be either of the same class as the specific cards or else unclassified. As there is only one class, (C), in which two general cards occur, the combination of two specific cards with two general cards of the same class is possible only in this department, namely, Opera.

2. Three specific cards of the same class, and one general card, which must be of the same class as the specific cards with which it is associated, or else an unclassified general card.

3. Four specific cards of the same class.

4. In grade 15, and during the continuation of this course, four unclassified general cards may be combined into a book having a value of 8.

This rule applies also to Grades 9 to 12 of the Normal Course.

5. No other combination is admitted as composing a book. Every book, except those under rule 4, must contain at least two specific cards.

6. As the exercise proceeds a book may be formed at any time by any one who may secure the requisite cards. It is discretionary, however, with those participating to form their books when they choose. Since all books are

not equally valuable, it is usually better to defer making up a book, even though there may be a sufficient number of cards of a class in the player's possession to render it possible, until he shall have secured certain cards which, when put together, will give the book the highest value attainable. This introduces an element of enterprise into the game, since by retaining the cards he incurs the danger of having them called from him. (See Sec. III.) When a book is formed, the possessor, when discarding it from his hand, must announce the subjects of the cards of which it is composed. Special attention should be given to this announcement, as otherwise the participants will incur the disadvantage of calling for cards already disposed of.

The player will do well in making up books before the end of the game, to take care and retain in his hand at least one specific card of every class, since without the aid of the list of titles at the top of these cards he will often be unable to recall the names of the cards he might ask for.

SECTION III. VALUE OF THE BOOKS.

Inasmuch as the game turns upon the points acquired by adding together the value of the different books that each player may be able to make up during the progress of the exercise, when the acquisition of cards ceases, (see Sec IV), the following principles of valuation are important.

1. Any book counts 1.
2. This valuation may be increased in two ways: 1st by agreements between the valuations on the specific cards, or 2nd by superior value of the classified general cards, as follows:

3. Two specific cards (of the same class) agreeing in one valuation of quality, adds 1 to the value of the book. The coincidence of two or more ciphers among valuations is not counted. The ciphers merely signify that the quality in connection with which they occur had not yet begun to appear in music. Only the significant figures are counted in estimating agreements of qualitative valuation.

4. Two specific cards agreeing in two valuations adds 2 to the value of the book.

5. Two specific cards agreeing in three qualities adds 3 to the value of the book.

6. And so on, adding 1 for every agreement of valuation between two specific cards.

7. Three specific cards agreeing in one valuation adds 2 to the value of the book.

8. Three specific cards agreeing in two valuations adds 4 to the value of the book.

9. Three specific cards agreeing in three valuations adds 6 to the value of the book.

10. And so on, adding 2 for every element of agreement between three specific cards in a book.

11. Four specific cards agreeing in one valuation constitute a book valued at 10. This combination is possible in every class except Class B.

12. A classified general card adds 1 to the value of a book.

13. Two classified general cards add 2 to the value of a book. Note.—This combination is possible only in Class C.

14. After grade 15 in the regular course, and in grades 9 to 12 of the normal course, any four unclassified general cards form a book, which is valued at 6,

15. Hence the value of a book is ascertained by adding to the 1 in rule 1 as many additional points as can be found for it under the remaining rules, with two exceptions, viz.: 1st, when a book is composed of four specific cards agreeing in the valuation of one quality, (see rule II, sec. III), its total value is 10; 2d, when a book is composed of four unclassified general cards, (see rule 14. sec. III), its total value is 6.

SECTION IV. HOW TO ACQUIRE THE CARDS.

1. As no advantage attaches to the privilege of dealing, it does not matter which one of the participants first performs this office. It may be determined by lot. After reducing the pack to the requirements of the grade, (Sec. V), and shuffling the cards well, the dealer gives each player in turn one card until each player has four. The remainder of the pack is placed face downwards in the center of the table.

2. All the players now inspect their cards, with a view of ascertaining what cards they can best employ to complete or advance a book, (Sec. II and III).

3. The player at the left of the dealer has the first call; he has the right to demand of any other player he may happen to select, a card, of a class of which he holds representatives in his hand. In case he is unfamiliar with the game, he will find at the top of nearly every specific card the titles of all the cards in the class. This will serve to prompt him. In calling a card he must conform to the requirements of the grade as to the class and the grade. (See Sec. V.) These requirements should be looked up in the accompanying volume, and placed where they can be readily consulted. If he asks for the card desired, in the form required in

the Grade of the Exercise, the holder is obliged to surrender it; proper asking in the higher grades includes the caller answering whatever question the grade may require, after the player called has acknowledged that he possesses the card. When the question is correctly answered, or the demands of the lower grades met, the card is surrendered. The caller then has the right to demand any other card he may desire from the same or any other player, the card being surrendered in every instance whenever the requirements of the grade have been complied with. When he demands a card which the player called does not hold, he must draw the top card from the pack; if this happens to be the card demanded from the last player called, he must show it to the participants, (to insure good faith), whereupon he has a right to call again from any player any other card desired. His right to call ceases whenever he fails to obtain the card called, either from the player or by drawing it from the pack.

4. The next player upon the left then has the right to call, which he may exercise upon any player among the participants, irrespective of order of precedence. His right to call ceases whenever he fails to obtain the desired card, either from the participant from whom he called it, or from the pack.

5. The acquisition of cards continues until the pack is exhausted, whereupon the players proceed to make up whatever combinations of books they are able from the cards in their possession. In doing this they will find considerable latitude for choice, in pursuit of more profitable combinations. The cards remaining in their hands uncombined are discarded. The results of the game are then computed for each player in turn, accord-

ing to the valuation of books in Sec. III. Of these a record must be kept in a book provided for the purpose, in order that the prizes may be properly awarded, and that the progress of the various players may be more accurately measured.

SECTION V.
REQUIREMENTS OF THE PROGRESSIVE GRADES.

As the prime object of these studies is that of mastering all the information embraced in all the 96 cards, (an amount of information equal to a good-sized volume) the just apportionment of this work among all the successive exercises of the course becomes important—indeed indispensable to success. The rapidity with which the class may advance will depend very materially upon the age of the students and their disposition with regard to devoting study to the preparation of the work for the next-coming grade. Hence it is impossible to prescribe any one exact course which ought under all circumstances to be followed. Accordingly we have devoted no small attention to the details of an elaborate course of over forty lessons, which will finally result in bringing out all the information upon the entire 96 cards without rendering the various steps onerous to average students of grammar grades in school. When the class consists of more advanced mental habits, such as those of the eighth grammar grade or the first year high school, the course may be shortened at the discretion of the teacher, by combining in a single meeting the information here apportioned to two or more successive grades. In place of this, when the interest and seriousness of the student warrants such a proceeding, the Normal course of twelve lessons may be followed. Observe that the same grade is continued throughout the evening or session of the class in which it was begun. As it only requires about fifteen minutes to go through the game once, during the hour or hour and a half of the session the same grade will be gone through with from five to six times, and in this way the information becomes more and more familiar. In advanced stages of the studies it will be optional with the teacher to conduct some of the later exercises of the session according to the requirements of an earlier grade, for the purpose of review.

In both these courses the first intention is that of making the student familiar with the general range of the subjects, the names and dates of the principal composers, and the names of his principal works in every department. Much is to be learned from handling the cards in this way, when as yet no information is required beyond the correct pronunciation of titles, names and the dates appertaining thereto. Through the mere effort to acquire cards, the student unconsciously is beguiled into knowing many things of general musical knowledge, which at the end of the proceeding he may not be able to remember having tried to learn. This process goes through the entire course; every lesson makes the player more and more familiar with the different provinces of musical effort covered by the exercise, and this while his main conscious attention is devoted to the specific information upon the new cards added latest to the pack in use.

Most of this general information is deducable from the upper parts of the cards; but as it is not possible to obtain a clue to the missing unclassified general cards in this way, they are not called from one player to another until after the first fifteen grades, by which time the players will have become familiar with most of them through frequent seeing. Every exercise is to be conducted strictly according to the following requirements, specific to the progressive grades in which the exercise is conducted.

Grade 1. The first eight grades are played with a part of a pack only, in order to render the student sooner familiar with the information. Begin by discarding from the pack all the cards of classes E, F, G and H, and the unclassified general cards not hereafter named. Take all the cards of classes A, B, C, D and the unclassified general cards, " Madrigal," " Mass," " Requiem," " Te Deum," " Principles of Pronunciation," "Principles of the Beautiful," "The Classical in Music" and "Definition of the Romantic." The eight unclassified general cards are not called from one player to another, but may be used in completing combinations for books, according to Secs. II and III. All other cards may be called from one player to another, according to the directions in Sec. IV, and the particular restrictions of the grade, as here following:

Requirements: Any card of classes A, B, C and D must be surrendered to the player asking for it, when mentioned by its proper title.

In making up books the players will need to consult Secs. II and III, in order to secure the greatest number of credits possible by fortunate combinations of cards they hold.

Grade 2. The pack remains the same as in the previous grade. There are no additional requirements, except that the pronunciation of names and titles used must be correct. The object of this grade is to still further familiarize the students with the general range of the information upon the cards.

In case of a demand being made upon one of the participants for a card which he holds, and the name or title being incorrectly pronounced, the card may be retained and not surrendered. If, however, the player have the card he must so state, and also give the ground for his refusal to surrender it; whereupon the caller must proceed to draw from the pack, exactly as if the card had not been in the hand of the player called. In case of a dispute as to the accuracy of the pronunciation, it must be repeated and put to vote of the entire number of participants, the phonetic spelling upon the cards serving as standard, the vote of a majority determining the point whether the card demanded should or should not have been surrendered. Contests of this kind are educational in their influence upon all concerned in the exercise.

Grade 3. The pack remains as in the previous exercises. Requirements: Classes A and B; in demanding a card of either of these classes the player must give also the date at the upper left hand corner of the card. Unless the date is given, the player need not surrender the card.

Classes C and D; the name of composer of work named upon the card asked for, belonging to these classes, must be given as well as the title. Correct pronunciation is required here and everywhere else through the remaining grades. Disputes are to be settled by appeal to the cards and a decision of the majority playing.

Grade 4. The pack remains as in the previous grades. Requirements: Classes A and B; both dates must be given (upper right and left hand corners). In classes C and D correct pronunciation of titles and composers' names of specific cards called. Disputes to be settled as before.

Grade 5. By this time the players have become familiar with the range of the cards, the subjects upon them and the principles of making books, and therefore the most effective manners of combining the cards accumulated during the acquisition of cards. It is now time to begin more formally upon the solid information which the cards were intended to convey. Hence the following requirements:

Classes A and B. Cards are surrendered only upon the caller being able to answer question No. 1 assigned to each card of these classes. Cards of Classes C and D will be surrendered only when the date and place of production of the work is given (except in the few instances where this information has not been embodied upon the cards.)

Note. It is not expected that the very words of the question in the book will be committed to memory. All that is asked is that the caller be able to answer any question covering the first point of information in the text upon the card. In case of a dispute between the caller and the called, the question must be restated, the answer given, and the corresponding part of the text of the card read aloud; a majority vote of the participants will determine whether the card shall or shall not be surrendered. Should the player holding the card demanded be unable to recall the question, or frame another requiring the same information for its full and correct answer, he must surrender the card.

Grade 6. The pack remains as before.

Requirements preliminary to surrendering cards: Classes A and B, the same as in the previous grade.

Classes C and D: the date of birth of composers mentioned.

Grade 7. The pack remains the same as before. Requirements: Classes A and B; give dates upon both upper corners, covering date of birth and death or the beginning and end of period to which the card is devoted.

Classes C and D. Dates of birth and death of composers. (For example: suppose the caller demands "Armide," Lulli, Class C, he must also give the dates of Lulli, namely 1633-1687. And so on in other cases. Where there is no date at the top of the card, as in some of the cards of Class B, the dates must be obtained from the body of the text. In case of cards devoted to more than one composer, the dates of the first will be sufficient in this grade).

Grade 8. The pack remains as before. Requirements: Before surrendering any card of Classes A, B, C and D, the player holding them has the right to demand of the caller that he answer the first question upon the card called, when properly asked.

It will be remembered that the first question was already applied to the cards in classes A and B in grades 5 and 6, hence the new matter in this grade comprises only the first questions upon the cards of classes C and D.

Grade 9. Add to the pack, previously in use, all the cards of class E and two unclassified general cards, namely, "The Fantasia" and "The Song without Words." These two latter, like all the other unclassified general cards, are not yet called from one player to another, but remain the property of the player acquiring them from the pack. Requirements: Cards of class E are surrendered only upon the caller giving correct pronunciation and the names and dates of composers. All other callable cards are surrendered, as in grade 8, upon the caller answering the first question relating to the text.

Grade 10. Add the cards of class F and two unclassified general cards, namely, "The Fugue" and "The Etude." Requirements: Cards of class F are surrendered when the demand is coupled with the name and dates of the composer of the work whose card is called. Classes A, B, C, D and E, only upon the ability of the caller to answer the first question upon the text.

Reward. At the tenth exercise a reward should be given to the student who has attained the greatest number of credits during the entire ten exercises. For this purpose a record must be kept and the credits of each successive exercise added to the total already attained. This reward should take the form of a valuable musical work, and in order that the expense of this part of the course may be as little as possible, the publishers have arranged to furnish suitable books for this purpose (only) at merely nominal prices.

Grade 11. Add to the pack used in the previous grade all the cards of class G and the two general cards "The Nocturne" and "Typical Musical Forms."

Requirements: Cards of Class G are surrendered only upon the caller giving names of composers, correct pronunciations and dates of birth and death of composers. Class F; the caller must be able to answer the first question. All other cards are surrendered upon answering the first question.

Grade 12. Add the cards of Class H and the general cards, "Literary Interpretations in Musical Æsthetics," and "Musical History and Why it should be Studied."

Requirements: Names and dates of composers upon Class H, and place and date of works to which the card is devoted when given on card. First question of all other cards.

Grade 13. Add the cards of Class I.

Requirements: Names and dates of composers of works on cards of Classes A, B, C, D, E, F, G. Class II, first question.

Grade 14. Requirements: Classes A and B second question; Classes C, D, E, F, G and H names and dates of composers; Class I, first question.

Grade 15. In this grade the unclassified general cards are made subject to call from one player to another, precisely the same as the specific cards. By this time the players ought to be familiar with the names of the unclassified general cards, from having often held them in their hands.

Requirements: Unclassified general cards will be surrendered only upon correctly answering the first question upon their subject matter. Cards of Classes A, B, C and D will be surrendered only upon correctly answering the second question on their text. Classes E, F, G, H and I, upon correctly giving the names and dates of the composers.

Grade 16. In the succeeding grades, Classes A, B, C and D, and Classes E, F, G and H, may be alternately omitted, thus avoiding an unnecessary repetition of questions and answers, and concentrating the attention more exclusively upon the new requirements which are introduced in each grade. This omission may not be practicable when eight or more persons are engaged, and in such instances all the cards may be retained. In the following grades it will be understood that when the word "*omit*" occurs before the statement of requirements, the classes to which those requirements refer, may be omitted.

Requirements: Classes A, B, C and D, (*omit*), answer the second question assigned to the card required.

Classes E, F, G and H, answers to first questions. Class I, and unclassified cards, answers to first questions.

Grade 17. Requirements: Classes A, B, C and D, (omit), same as in Grade 16. E, F, G, H and I, *answer to second question*. Unclassified cards, same as in Grade 15.

Grade 18. Requirements: Classes A, B, C and D, (omit), same as in Grade 16. E, F, G and H, same as in Grade 17. I and unclassified cards, *correct answer to second question*.

Grade 19. Requirements: Classes A, B, C and D, *answer to third question*. E, F, G and H, (omit), same as in Grade 17. I and unclassified cards, same as in Grade 18.

Grade 20. In this and in all subsequent grades, both *Classified General Cards*, and *Unclassified General Cards*, can only be exchanged *three times* upon the requirements assigned. After a card of the above mentioned kinds, has changed hands three times, it shall remain in the possession of the player last acquiring it unless the correct answer to the question next following the one assigned in this grade be given. For example, *Characterization of Opera*, may be exchanged but three times in the present grade upon the third question, What purpose is served by the Recitative? being correctly asked and answered, but it may continue to be exchanged if the fourth question, What is expressed in the Arias? be answered. The continued possession of the card depends, however, upon its possessor being able to *ask* the next question as a means of defense. Should the card be demanded of him a fourth time, he must surrender it upon the correct answer to the *third* question being given, unless he is able to ask the *fourth* question, when his opponent must answer it correctly before he can secure the card. The card may then change hands any number of times upon the question next following the one assigned in this grade being properly asked and correctly answered, and the rule applies to all the following grades of the entire course. *Should participants so mutually desire and agree the above rule may apply to all the cards.*

Requirements: Classes A, B, C and D, (omit), same as in Grade 19. E, F, G and H, *answer to third question.* I and unclassified cards, same as in Grade 18.

Grade 21. Requirements: Classes A, B, C and D, same as Grade 19. E, F, G and H, (omit), same as in Grade 20. I and unclassified cards, *answer to third question.*

Grade 22. Requirements: Classes A, B, C and D, *answer to fourth question.* E, F, G and H, (omit), same as in Grade 20. I and unclassified cards same as in Grade 21.

Grade 23. Requirements: Classes A, B, C and D, (omit), same as in Grade 22. E, F, G and H, *answer to fourth question.* I and unclassified cards same as in Grade 21.

Grade 24. Requirements: Classes A, B, C and D, same as in Grade 22. E, F, G and H, (omit), same as in Grade 23. I and unclassified cards *answer to fourth question.*

Grade 25. Requirements: Classes A, B, C and D, *answer to fifth question.* E, F, G and H, (omit), same as in Grade 23. I and unclassified cards, same as in Grade 24.

Grade 26. Requirements: Classes A, B, C and D, (omit), same as in Grade 25. E, F, G and H, *answer to fifth question.* I and unclassified cards, same as Grade 24.

Grade 27. Requirements: Classes A, B, C and D, same as in Grade 25. E, F, G and H, (omit), same as in Grade 26. I and unclassified cards *answer to fifth question*.

Grade 28. In this grade for the purpose of testing the memory and affording a slight review the possessor of a card may ask and demand an answer to any one of the first five questions before surrendering the card. The teacher or players may introduce this diversion as often as may seem desirable. Requirements: Classes A, B, C, D, E. F, G, H, I and unclassified cards, *answer to any one of the first five questions which the holder of a card may chose to present.*

Grade 29. Requirements: Classes A, B, C and D, *answer to sixth question*. E, F, G and H, (omit), same as in Grade 26. I and unclassified cards, same as in Grade 27.

Grade 30. Prize Awarded. Requirements: Classes A, B, C and D, (omit), same as in Grade 29. E, F, G and H, *answer to sixth question*. I and unclassified cards, same as in Grade 27.

Grade 31. Requirements: Classes A, B, C and D. same as in Grade 29. E, F, G and H (omit), same as in Grade 30. I and unclassified cards *answer to sixth question*.

Grade 32. As the questions assigned to the different cards vary in number, and as it is necessary to retain all cards of a class until nearly all of the questions have been presented, the players are at liberty to ask *any* question upon a card *whose list of questions has been exhausted.* It will, therefore, be understood that when the grade requires answers to the seventh question of Class C, or any other class, that it refers only to those cards which have not yet been exhausted, while to secure any other card the applicant must answer *any* question in the list which the holder may chose to present.

Requirements: Classes A, B, C and D, *answer seventh question*. E, F, G and H, (omit), same as in Grade 30. I and unclassified cards, same as in Grade 31.

Grade 33. Requirements: Classes A, B, C and D, (omit), same as in Grade 32. E, F, G and H, *answer seventh question*. I and unclassified cards, same as in Grade 31.

Grade 34. It will be observed that the questions upon several of the opera cards are already exhausted. Where this is the case the holder of a card may ask any question in its list and demand the correct answer before surrendering the card. Requirements: Classes A, B, C and D, same as in Grade 32. E, F, G and H, (omit), same as in Grade 33. I and unclassified cards, *answer to seventh question*.

Grade 35. Requirements: Classes A, B, C and D, *answer to eighth question*. E, F, G and H, (omit), same as in Grade 33. I and unclassified cards, same as in Grade 34.

Grade 36. Requirements: Classes A, B, C and D, (omit), same as in Grade 35. E, F, G and H *answer to eighth question* I and unclassified cards, same as in Grade 34.

Grade 37. Requirements: Classes A, B, C and D, same as in Grade 35. E, F, G and H, (omit), same as in Grade 36. I and unclassified cards, *answer to eighth question*.

Grade 38. Requirements: Classes A, B, C and D, *answer to ninth question*. E, F, G and H, (omit), same as in Grade 36. I and unclassified cards, same as in Grade 37.

Grade 39. Requirements: Classes A, B, C and D, (omit), same as in Grade 38. E, F, G and H *answer to ninth question*. I and unclassified cards, same as in Grade 37.

Grade 40. Requirements: Classes A, B, C and D, same as in Grade 38. E, F, G and H, (omit), same as in Grade 39. I and unclassified cards, *answer to ninth question*.

Grade 41. Requirements: Classes A, B, C and D, *answer to tenth question*. E, F, G and H, (omit), same as in Grade 39. I and unclassified cards, same as in Grade 40.

Grade 42. Requirements: Classes A, B, C and D, (omit), same as in Grade 41. E, F, G and H *answer to tenth question*. I and unclassified cards, same as in Grade 40.

Grade 43. Requirements: Classes A, B, C and D, same as in Grade 41. E, F, G and H, (omit), same as in Grade 42. I and unclassified cards, *answer to tenth question*.

Grade 44. As the lists of questions upon many of the cards are already exhausted it will be much easier to meet the requirements which follow than it has been to meet those of the preceding grades. Requirements: Classes A, B, C, D and E *answer to eleventh question* when there *is* an *eleventh* question and when there is not answer *any* question in the list corresponding to the card asked for which the holder may choose to present. F, G, H, I and unclassified cards *answer to tenth question*.

Grade 45. Requirements: Classes A, B, C, D and E, same as in Grade 44. F, G, H, I and unclassified cards, *answer to eleventh question*.

Grade 46. Requirements: Classes A, B, C, D and

E, *answer to twelfth question.* F, G, H, I and unclassified cards, same as in Grade 45.

Grade 47. Requirements: Classes A, B, C, D, and E, same as in Grade 46. F, G, H, I and unclassified cards, *answer to twelfth question.*

Grade 48. Requirements: Classes A, B, C, D and E, *answer to thirteenth question.* F, G, H, I and unclassified cards, same as in Grade 47.

Grade 49. Requirements: Classes A, B, C, D and E, same as in Grade 48. F, G, H, I and unclassified cards, *answer to thirteenth question.*

Grade 50. Requirements: Classes A, B, C, D, E, F, G, H, I and unclassified cards, *answer to fourteenth question*, or if there be no fourteenth question, then answer to *any* question relating to the card called.

Grade 51. Requirements: Include all classes. *Answer to the fifteenth question* when such occurs, and when it does not, to any question in the list corresponding to the card asked for.

Grade 52. Omit all of the cards belonging to Classes C and H. Requirements: *Answer to sixteenth question* upon remaining cards.

Grade 53. Requirements: *Answer to seventeenth question* upon remaining cards.

Grade 54. Omit Class A. Requirements: *Answer to eighteenth question* upon remaining cards.

Grade 55. In the remaining grades it is desired to exhaust the questions yet unanswered, and as the players are priviliged to ask *any* question whatsoever, and demand a correct answer before surrendering the card to which it relates, it is not improbable that all will acquire the additional information. Without it a player cannot hope to secure the cards desired if an opponent is able to fortify himself by asking one of the remaining questions.

Requirements: *Answer to any question which the possessor of a card may choose to ask, regardless of whether it has already been used or not.*

 Grade 56. Requirements: *Same as in Grade 55.*
 Grade 57. *Include cards of all classes* in the remaining grades. Requirements: *Same as in Grade 55.*
 Grade 58. Requirements: *Same as in Grade 55.*
 Grade 59. Requirements: *Same as in Grade 55.*
 Grade 60. Requirements: *Same as in Grade 55.*

PRIZES AWARDED.—As suggested in another place, where classes are organized it will be found advantageous to award prizes at intervals, as they are an incentive to study and an appropriate recognition of merit. Should the Manual of Music or Elson's Reminiscences of a Musician's Vacation Abroad be desired the publishers will furnish them, for this purpose only, at a special reduction.

SUMMARY OF REQUIREMENTS.

IN THE

PROGRESSIVE GRADES OR EXERCISES.

REGULAR COURSE.

1st Grade.
> Classes A, B, C and D. *No requirements.* Cards must be surrendered when called *regardless of correct pronunciation.* (See Instructions, page 133).

2nd Grade.
> Classes A, B, C and D *Titles and names* necessarily used to indicate cards desired *must b correctly pronounced.* (See Instructions, pages 133 and 134.)

3rd Grade.
> Classes A and B. Give date upper *left* hand corner of card.
> Classes C and D. Give title of work and *name of composer* but *correct pronunciation* if the *latter* is not yet required. (See Instructions, page 134.)

4th Grade.
> Classes A and B. Give *both* dates upper *left* and *right* corner of card.
> Classes C and D. Give title of work and name of composer and *pronounce both correctly.* (See Instructions, page 134).

5th Grade.
> Classes A and B. Answer correctly question No 1 assigned to the card required.
> Classes C and D. State *when* and *where* the work represented upon the card demanded was produced; as for example: Peri's *Eurydice*, Florence, 1600. (See Instructions, page 135.)

SUMMARY OF REQUIREMENTS.

6th Grade.
Classes A and B. *Review 5th Grade*; answer correctly ques. No 1 assigned to the card required.
Classes C and D. Give *date* of *birth* (upper left corner) of composer represented upon card demanded. Correct pronunciation of *both name and title now and hereafter always required in these classes.* Card may be retained even if date of birth be correctly given, if pronunciation is incorrect. (See Instructions page 135.)

7th Grade.
Classes A and B. *Review 4th Grade.* Give *both dates* upper left and right hand corners of cards.
Classes C and D. Give *both* dates—*birth* and *death* of composer, as for example: Peri 1550-1608. (See Instructions page 136.)

8th Grade.
Classes A and B. *Review 5th Grade*; answer correctly *ques. No. 1* assigned to the card required.
Classes C and D. Answer correctly *ques. No. 1* assigned to the card required. (See Instructions page 136.)

NOTE: Add to cards already in use, all of CLASS E SYMPHONY and the "unclassified general cards" *Fantasia* and *Song Without Words.*

9th Grade
Classes A, B, C and D. *Review 8th Grade*; answer correctly ques. No. 1 assigned to the card required.
Class E. Give *correct pronunciation* of *names* of composers and *dates* of *birth* and *death*. (See Instructions, page 136).

NOTE: Add to cards already in use all of CLASS F, CONCERTO, and the "unclassified general cards" *Fugue* and *Qualities of Etudes.*

10th Grade.
Classes A, B, C and D. *Review 8th Grade.* Answer correctly ques. No. 1 assigned to the card required.
Class E. Answer correctly ques. No. 1 assigned to the card required.
Class F. Give *correct pronunciation* of *names* of composers and *dates* of *birth* and *death*. (PRIZE AWARDED. Read carefully Instructions, page 136).

NOTE: Add to cards already in use all of CLASS G, SONATA, and the "unclassified general cards" *Nocturne* and *Typical Musical Forms.*

11

SUMMARY OF REQUIREMENTS.

11th Grade.
Classes A, B, C, D and E. *Review.* Answer correctly ques. No. 1 assigned to the card required. [Note: If preferred the requirements in these classes in this grade may consist of a review of the dates instead of the first question.]
Class F. Answer correctly ques. No. 1 assigned to the card required.
Class G. Give *correct pronunciation* of *names* of composers and *dates of birth* and *death.* (See Instructions, page 137).

NOTE: Add to cards already in use all of CLASS H, CHAMBER MUSIC, and the "unclassified general cards" *Literary Interpretation in Musical Æsthetics* and *The History of Music; Reasons Why it Should be Studied.*

12th Grade.
Classes A, B, C, D, E and F *Review.* Answer ques. No. 1 assigned to the card required. [Note: If preferred the requirements in these classes in this grade may consist of a *review of dates in Classes A and B* and of *time* and *place of production* of works *when given upon the cards* in Classes C, D, E and F]
Class G. Answer correctly question No. 1 assigned to the card required.
Class H. Give *correct pronunciation* of *names* of composers, dates of birth and death and time and place of works when given on the cards. [Note: This requirement may be abridged at the discretion of the teacher or participants if too difficult. See Instructions, page 137.]

NOTE: Add to cards already in use all of CLASS I, SONG.

13th Grade.
Classes A, B, C, D, E, F and G. Give correct pronunciation of names and dates of birth and death of composers.
Class H. Answer correctly ques. No. 1 assigned to the card required.
Class I. Give *correct pronunciation* of *names* of composers and *dates of birth* and *death.*

14th Grade.
Classes A and B. Answer correctly ques. No. 2 assigned to the card required.
Classes C, D, E, F, G and H. Give names and dates of composers.
Class I. Answer correctly ques. No. 1 assigned to the card required.

NOTE: In this and all subsequent grades the "unclassified general cards" may be called at will from one to the other. (See Instructions, page 138).

SUMMARY OF REQUIREMENTS.

15th Grade.
- Classes A and B. Answer ques. No. 2.
- Classes C and D. Answer ques. No. 2.
- Classes E, F, G, H and I. Give names and dates of composers.
- Unclassified cards, give correct answer to ques. No. 1 assigned to the card required.

16th Grade.
- Classes A, B, C and D. Omit.
- Classes E, F, G and H. Answer to ques No. 1.
- Class I and unclassified cards. Answer ques. No. 1. (See Instructions, page 138)

17th Grade.
- Classes A, B, C and D. Omit.
- Classes E, F, G, H and I. Answer ques. No. 2.
- Unclassified cards. Answer ques. No. 1.

18th Grade.
- Classes A, B, C and D. Omit.
- Classes E, F, G and H. Answer ques. No. 2.
- Class I and unclassified cards. Answer to ques. No. 2.

19th Grade.
- Classes A, B, C and D. Answer ques. No. 3.
- Classes E, F, G and H. Omit.
- Class I and unclassified cards. Answer to ques. No. 2.

20th Grade.
- Classes A, B, C and D. Omit.
- Classes E, F, G, and H. Answer ques. No. 3.
- Class I and unclassified cards. Answer ques. No 2. (Read carefully Instructions, pages 139 and 140).

21st Grade.
- Classes A, B, C and D. Answer ques. No. 4.
- Classes E, F, G and H. Omit.
- Class I and unclassified cards. Answer to ques. No. 4.

22nd Grade.
- Classes A, B, C and D. Answer ques. No. 4.
- Classes E, F, G and H. Omit.
- Class I and unclassified cards. Answer ques. No. 3.

23rd Grade.
- Classes A, B, C and D. Omit.
- Classes E, F, G and H. Answer ques. No. 4.
- Class I and unclassified cards. Answer to ques. No. 3.

24th Grade.
- Classes A, B, C and D. Answer ques. No. 4.
- Classes E, F, G and H. Omit.
- Class I and unclassified cards. Answer to ques. No. 4.

25th Grade.
- Classes A, B, C and D. Answer ques. No. 5.
- Classes E, F, G and H. Omit.
- Class I and unclassified cards. Answer to ques. No. 4.

SUMMARY OF REQUIREMENTS.

26th Grade.
- Classes A, B, C and D. Omit.
- Classes E, F, G and H. Answer ques. No. 5.
- Class I and unclassified cards. Answer to ques. No. 4.

27th Grade.
- Classes A, B, C and D. Answer ques. No. 5.
- Classes E, F, G and H. Omit.
- Class I and unclassified cards. Answer to ques. No. 5.

28th Grade.
- Classes A, B, C and D. Answer question No 1, 2, 3, 4 or 5 as required.
- Class E, F, G and H. Answer question No 1, 2, 3, 4 or 5 as required.
- Class I and unclassified cards. Answer to ques. No. 1, 2, 3, 4 or 5 as required. (See Instructions, Grade 28, page 141.)

29th Grade.
- Classes A, B, C and D. Answer ques. No. 6.
- Classes E, F, G and H. Omit.
- Class I and unclassified cards. Answer to ques. No. 5.

30th Grade.
- Classes A, B, C and D. Prize Awarded. Omit.
- Classes E, F, G and H. Answer ques. No. 6.
- Class I and unclassified cards. Answer to ques. No. 5.

31st Grade.
- Classes A, B, C and D. Answer ques. No. 6.
- Classes E, F, G and H. Omit.
- Class I and unclassified cards. Answer to ques. No. 6.

32nd Grade.
- Classes A, B, C and D. Answer ques. No. 7.
- Classes E, F, G and H. Omit.
- Class I and unclassified cards. Answer to ques. No. 6. (See Instructions, Grade 32, page 142.)

33rd Grade.
- Classes A, B, C and D. Omit.
- Classes E, F, G and H. Answer ques. No. 7.
- Class I and unclassified cards. Answer to ques. No. 6.

34th Grade.
- Classes A, B, C and D. Answer ques. No. 7.
- Classes E, F, G and H. Omit.
- Class I and unclassified cards. Answer to ques. No. 7. (See Instructions, Grade 34, page 142.)

35th Grade.
- Classes A, B, C and D. Answer ques. No. 8.
- Classes E, F, G and H. Omit.
- Class I and unclassified cards. Answer to ques. No. 7.

SUMMARY OF REQUIREMENTS. 151

36th Grade.
- Classes A, B, C and D. Omit.
- Classes E, F, G and H. Answer ques. No. 8.
- Class I and unclassified cards. Answer to ques. No. 7.

37th Grade.
- Classes A, B, C and D. Answer ques. No. 8.
- Classes E, F, G and H. Omit.
- Class I and unclassified cards. Answer to ques. No. 8.

38th Grade.
- Classes A, B, C, and D Answer ques. No. 9.
- Classes E, F, G and H. Omit.
- Class I and unclassified cards. Answer to ques. No. 8.

39th Grade.
- Classes A, B, C and D. Omit.
- Classes E, F, G and H. Answer ques. No. 9.
- Class I and unclassified cards. Answer to ques. No. 8.

40th Grade.
- Classes A, B, C and D. Answer ques. No. 9.
- Classes E, F, G and H. Omit.
- Class I and unclassified cards. Answer to ques. No. 9.

41st Grade.
- Classes A, B, C and D. Answer ques. No. 10.
- Classes E, F, G and H. Omit.
- Class I and unclassified cards. Answer to ques. No. 9.

42nd Grade.
- Classes A, B, C and D Omit.
- Classes E, F, G and H. Answer ques. No. 10.
- Class I and unclassified cards. Answer to ques. No. 9.

43rd Grade.
- Classes A, B, C and D. Answer ques. No. 10.
- Classes E, F, G and H. Omit.
- Class I and unclassified cards. Answer to ques. No. 10.

44th Grade.
- Classes A, B, C, D and E. Answer ques. No. 11.
- Classes F, G, H, I and unclassified cards. Answer ques No. 10. (See Instructions, Grade 44, page 143.)

45th Grade.
- Classes A, B, C, D and E. Answer ques. No. 11.
- F, G, H, I and unclassified cards. Answer ques. No. 11.

46th Grade.
- Classes A, B, C, D and E. Answer ques. No. 12.
- F, G, H, I and unclassified cards. Answer ques. No. 11.

SUMMARY OF REQUIREMENTS.

47th Grade. { Classes A, B, C, D and E. Answer ques. No. 12.
F, G, H, I and unclassified cards. Answer ques. No. 12.

48th Grade. { Classes A, B, C, D and E. Answer ques. No. 13.
F, G, H, I and unclassified cards. Answer ques. No. 12.

49th Grade. { Classes A, B, C, D and E. Answer ques. No. 13.
F, G, H, I and unclassified cards. Answer ques. No. 13.

50th Grade, { Include all of the cards. Answer ques. No. 14. (See Instructions, page 144.)

51st Grade. { Include all of the cards. Answer ques. No. 15. (See Instructions, page 144.)

52nd Grade. { *Omit* classes C and H. Answer ques, No. 16 on remaining cards.

53rd Grade. { Answer ques. No. 17 upon remaining cards.

54th Grade. { *Omit Class A*. Answer question No. 18 upon remaining cards.

55th Grade. { Answer to any ques. asked relating to card called for. (See Instructions, p. 144.)

Grades 56, 57, 58, 59 & 60. { Repeat the requirements of 55th Grade.

NORMAL COURSE.

COMPLETING THE STUDIES IN TWELVE LESSONS.

In order to meet the wishes of advanced students desiring to master the outlines of musical history in the smallest practicable number of lessons, the following system of progressive grades has been devised, based upon a special series of questions, four to each card, so planned as to elicit their entire contents. As there are 96 cards in the pack, even this small number of questions will afford no less than 384 questions, besides the names and dates at the top of the cards. It will therefore be impossible to master the information within the limits here proposed unless considerable preparatory study is given each exercise. The average of questions will be about thirty-three at each exercise, and it is not far from accurate to say that the matter necessary to master, in order to answer them fairly, will be equal to about eight or ten pages of a high-school text-book. This amount of matter is not a long lesson for any high-school pupil, and the conditions of emulation and the vicissitudes of the game will render the exercise interesting in spite of the amount of work it contains. In order to conduct the Normal Course successfully, the following directions in regard to the cards used and the requirements of each grade must be scrupulously observed.

Grade 1. Begin with a partial pack, embracing all of Classes A, B, C, D, and the unclassified general cards, "Mass," "Requiem," "Te Deum," "Principles of the beautiful," "The Classical in Music," "The Romantic in Music," "Rules of Pronunciation," and "Literary Interpretation in Musical Æthetics."

The eight unclassified general cards are not called from one player to another until Grade 9. They remain with the player obtaining them from the pack until combined in books, according to the rules in Sec. II.

Deal one card to each player in turn, until each has four. Place the remainder of the pack used face downwards, at a convenient place upon the table. The player upon the left of the dealer has the first right to call from any other player he may select, whatever card he may desire for completing or advancing a "book," the same as directed in Sec. IV.

Requirements in Grade 1. No card need be surrendered by the player from whom it has been called unless the caller give, beside the title of the card, the name of the composer and the dates of birth and death. Cards of Classes A and B, not being devoted to specific works, must be claimed by giving the dates of the persons and period as found upon the upper corners of the cards, or in the body of the text. These dates and the names of the composers may be given by the caller at first, or he may only give the title of the card, whereupon the holder may demand the remaining information here required before surrendering it. If the card is not held by the player from whom it has been called, the player draws the top card from the pack, as in Sec. IV. If the card, however, is not surrendered for want of the explicit information here designated, the caller forfeits his privilege of drawing from the pack. Then the player next upon his left has the privilege of calling, upon the same conditions.

Grade 2. The pack remains as before, Classes A, B, C, D, and the eight unclassified general cards mentioned in Grade 1. Requirements: Cards are called by their titles, and if devoted to particular works, the name of the composer must be added. If the player from whom the demand is made holds the card called, he will not surrender it until the first question concerning this card in the Normal Course has been fairly answered. In case of dispute as to the sufficiency of answers, the decision is made as explained in Sec. V.

Grade 3. The pack remains as before. Requirements: Cards are called as in the previous grade, but the holder will not surrender them until the 2nd question of the Normal Course has been answered sufficiently.

Grade 4. The pack remains as before. Requirements: The caller must answer the 3d question of the Normal Course before the card will be surrendered.

Grade 5. Add to the pack in use in the earlier grades all the cards of Classes E, F and G, and the following unclassified general cards: "Fugue," "Fantasie," "Nocturne," "Song Without Words," "Madrigal" and "Musical History." Requirements: Classes E, F and G will not be surrendered unless the names and dates of composers are given. Classes A and B require the 4th question of the Normal Course to be answered. Classes C and D still remain at the 3d question. (Note. At the discretion of the teacher, one of the earlier questions may be substituted in these classes in this grade, for the sake of review.)

Grade 6. The pack remains as in Grade 5. Requirements: Classes E, F G, 1st questions of Normal Course. Class C, 4th question. Class A and B any question of the Normal Course which the teacher or the class may agree upon at commencing the game. (This will have the force of a review in these classes.)

Grade 7. Pack remains as in Grade 5. Requirements: Classes E, F and G, 2nd question of the Normal Course. Class D, 4th question of Normal Course. Classes A, B and C, any question which the class may have agreed upon at the beginning of the exercise.

Grade 8. Add the cards of Classes H and I, and the remaining unclassified cards. Requirements: Classes H and I, names and dates of composers. Classes E, F, G, 3d question of Normal Course. Classes A, B, C, D, names and dates of composers, or dates of periods in Class B.

Grade 9. In this grade the general unclassified cards, for the first time, are called from one player to another, exactly like all others. For this reason they acquire a special value in this and the following grades of the course. See Sec. III, 14. Requirements: Unclassified general cards, the 1st question of the Normal Course. Classes E, F, G, 4th question of Normal Course. Classes H and I, 1st question of Normal Course. Classes A, B, C, D, 1st question.

Grade 10. Full pack. General cards, unclassified, subject to call. Requirements: Unclassified general cards and Classes H and I, 2d question of Normal Course. Classes A, B, C, D, E, F and G, 2d question of Normal Course.

Grade 11. Pack the same as in preceding grade. Requirements, 3rd question of Normal course in all classes.

Grade 12. Full pack. Call general cards. Requirements: 4th question of all classes, Normal Course.

It will be seen that in this course the entire information upon the first seven classes is gone through and reviewed, as also are the names and dates of composers. Should the teacher care to carry on the course a little longer, the unclassified general cards may be restored to the position which they occupied in the first seven grades, remaining with the player acquiring them from the pack. All other cards may be surrendered upon correctly answering whatever question of the course may have been selected at the beginning of the exercise, or two questions may be required. After two exercises of this kind the unclassified general cards may be restored to the rank they have in grades 9 to 12, and all four of the Normal Course questions required as condition to surrendering them. In these later exercises the knowledge of the players will by no means remain stationary, but on the contrary will now become more thorough in respect to the valuations, and the relations of different works of the same class to each other. This will be an incidental result of the effort of the players to effect more and more valuable combinations. The honorable completion and review of the Normal Course should be recognized by suitable tokens to the one or two players having acquired the highest number of credits.

SUMMARY OF REQUIREMENTS.

IN THE

PROGRESSIVE GRADES OR EXERCISES.

NORMAL COURSE.

NOTE: As it is manifestly impossible to plan a course which will be equally well adapted to pupils of various degrees of aptitude and proficiency, the author relies upon the teacher to make any changes in the apportionment of requirements which may be deemed necessary to render the course thoroughly practical and efficient. It may be found expedient to extend the Normal Course through a greater number of Exercises, but of this the teacher or class must be the judge.

1st GRADE.
{ Classes A and B. Give dates upper right and left hand corner of cards.
Classes C and D. Give title of work, name of composer, and dates of birth and death. (See Instructions, page 153 and 154.)

2nd GRADE.
{ Classes A and B. Answer question No. 1 relating to the card required.
Classes C and D. Give title of work and name of composer, pronouncing both correctly. Also answer ques. No, 1 relating to the card required.

3rd GRADE.
{ Classes A and B. Answer ques. No. 2.
Classes C and D. Answer ques. No. 2.

4th Grade.
{ Classes A and B. Answer ques. No. 3.
Classes C and D. Answer ques. No. 3.

NOTE: Add all cards of Classes E, F and G, and six unclassified general cards. (See Instructions, page 155.)

SUMMARY OF REQUIREMENTS. 159

5th Grade.
- Classes A and B. Answer ques. No. 4.
- Classes A and D. Answer ques. No. 3.
- Classes E, F and G. Give dates of birth and death.

6th Grade.
- Classes A and B. Answer to ques. No. 1, 2, 3 or 4, as teacher or class may decide
- Class C. Answer to ques. No. 4.
- Class D. Answer ques. No. 3.
- Classes E, F and G. Answer ques. No. 1.

7th Grade.
- Classes A, B and C. Answer to ques. No. 1, 2, 3 or 4 as teacher or class may decide.
- Class D. Answer ques. No. 4.
- Class E, F and G. Answer ques. No. 2.

Note. Add all of remaining cards.

8th Grade.
- Classes A, B, C and D. Give dates upper right and left hand corners of cards.
- Classes E, F and G. Answer ques. No. 3.
- Classes H and I. Give dates of birth and death.

9th Grade.
- Classes A, B, C and D. Answer question No 1.
- Classes E, F and G. Answer ques. No. 4.
- Classes H and I. Answer ques. No. 1.
- Unclassified cards. Answer ques. No. 1.

10th Grade. { Answer ques No. 2 upon all the cards.
11th Grade. { Answer ques. No. 3 upon all the cards,
12th Grade. { Answer ques. No. 4 upon all the cards,

SUPPLEMENTARY RULES AND SUGGESTIONS.

1. When a player having, (originally), only general cards in his hand, has no list of titles to guide him in calling, he may use his privilege of drawing from the pack *before* asking for cards.

2. It frequently becomes possible to form a book when by doing so the player will suffer a disadvantage, by using all the cards in his hand which have the list of titles upon them. In such instances, as he voluntarily incurs this disadvantage for the purpose of acquiring a book, he must abide by the consequences and lose his call.

3. When a book is formed, the class, names of composers, and if demanded the titles of works upon the cards used, must be distinctly announced. As the "unclassified general cards" are not subject to call until after the 15th grade in the Regular Course, and the 9th grade in the Normal Course, it is unnecessary to announce them before those grades. In announcing cards it will be found most satisfactory to all the players to have the class, and names of composers given instead of titles, as they are more easily remembered, thus: "Class E, Symphony, Beethoven, Schubert, Liszt and an unclassified card."

4. A player may be privileged to look at his own "books" at any time, should he forget what he has dis-

carded, but has no right to demand such information from his opponents.

5. When a player wishes to form a book, he must so announce before the player next following has called. After he has drawn from the pack, and his opponent has called, he has forfeited his right to form a book until after his next call.

6. When a player announces his intention of forming a book, he must announce the class at once, and if the player next following does not wish to call any cards from that class, he may proceed to call others, thus avoiding delay. But having once announced the intention of forming a book in a certain class, the player so announcing must form the book, as such an announcement unfulfilled is misleading. Failing to form a book after having so announced, a player forfeits his next call, and can only draw from the pack at his turn.

7. No cards are to be called after the last card has been drawn from the table. Players must then form all books possible from the cards in their possession. *After all books possible have been formed*, each player must place all cards still remaining in his possession, text upwards, on the table within plain view of all the players. The player who is found to *still have the largest number of cards of any class* shall be entitled to *all* the cards of *that class* held by *all other players*. Should two or more players have an *equal* number of cards, then the right of possession depends upon the total valuations of the first quality in the qualitative analysis nearest to the top of cards. For example should A have the two cards of Class C *Tristan and Isolde* and *The Hugenots* and B the two cards *Fidelio* and *Teodora*, A would be entitled to the cards because the valuation of "Musical Fitness"

which is the first quality in the table of opera is ten in one and eight in the other of the two first cards mentioned aggregating eighteen while in the two latter cards it is marked respectively seven and three, in total ten. The players holding an equal number of cards at this point will thus add together the valuations of the first quality and the one who has the highest total number shall be entitled to all the cards of that class. In case any two or more players find upon addition that their numbers are equal the valuations of the *second* quality in the table are to be used to determine the right of possession in exactly the same manner. The "unclassified general cards" are not to be exchanged but remain permanently in the possession of the players holding them when the last card is drawn from the table. After each player has obtained all the cards to which he is entitled through this process, additional books may be formed and the exercise finally closed. This method may be adopted or not at the option of the participants but the point must be decided at the beginning of the exercise.

PRONOUNCING DICTIONARY

OF

NAMES, TERMS AND PHRASES USED IN THE STUDIES.

Completeness has been no part of the design of this dictionary, it being essentially supplementary to the present Studies. Its object is to furnish pronunciations, definitions, explanations, etc., of words contained in the text of the cards, which might not be readily understood and correctly pronounced by the younger pupils.

If the simplicity and common usage of certain words would seem to preclude the necessity of pronouncing and defining them here, the reader will generously attribute this fact to the earnest desire of the author to adapt the Studies to the use of very young pupils, (and some who are well advanced in years are very young in music), to render every word, phrase and sentence thoroughly intelligible to all.

ā as in *ale*, ă *add*, ä *arm*, ē *eve*, ĕ *end*, ī *ice*, ĭ *ill*, o *old*, ŏ *odd*, oo *moon*, ü *bute*, u *but*. ü *French sound*, like e in *dew*.

Adagio, (ä-dä'-jĕ-o). A very slow degree of movement. Its original meaning was a rate of speed convenient to the player, hence, gradually its present meaning.

Agnus Dei, (äg'-nus dā'-ē). Lamb of God. One of the musical anthems in the mass.

A la Champetre, (ä lä-chäm-pātr'). Out of doors.

Allegro, (äl-lā'-gro). Rapid movement; cheerful.

Allegro Moderato, (äl-lā'-gro mŏd ĕ rä' to). Moderately quick.
Allegro Scherzando, (äl-lā'-gro skĕr-tsän'.do). Quick and playful; lively; merry.
Alma Redemptori, (äl'-mä rĕ-dĕm-to'-rē). A hymn to the virgin.
Amateur, (am'-ä-tur). One who has taste for music, but does not practice it as a profession; a dilettánte.
Ambrosian Scales. The four *modes* or scales adapted by St. Ambrose, Bishop of Milan, from the ancient Greek system. See St. Gregory the Great and his Reforms, Class A, Antiquities of Music.
Andante, (än-dän'-tĕ). Rather slow. Frequently combined with qualifying words.
Andantino. (än-dän-tē'-no). Slower than andante.
Antiphonary, (an-tĭf'-fo-nā-ry). Book of anthems, responses, etc., in the Catholic church.
Antiphonarium, (an'-tĭ-fo-nä'-rĭ-um). The collection of Antiphons used in the Catholic church; they are sung responsively by the priest and congregation or by two choirs.
Arezzo, (ä-rĕt'-so). A Tuscan city on the Chiana.
Aria, (ä'-rē-ä). An air; a song, sung by a single voice with or without an accompaniment. (See Class I, Definition of Qualities and Characterization of Song, and Class C, Characterization of Opera).
Arpeggio, (är-pād'-jē-o). A broken chord, the notes being played successively instead of simultaneously. Arpeggios begin with lowest tone, the left hand first then the right, upon completion of the left.
Aryan, (ar'-ĭ-än). An inhabitant of ancient Persia.
Aristotle, (ar'-ĭs-tŏt-l); b. Stagira in Macedonia, 384 B. C; d. 322 B. C. An eminent Greek philosopher. The first observer of musical phenomena by ear. (See Class A, Ancient Greek Music.)
Aristoxenos, (ar-ĭs-tok'-sä-no). A pupil of Aristotle, and a celebrated musical theorist. His doctrine of harmony is directly opposed to that of the Pythagoreans, according to whom musical concord depended upon certain mathematical ratios. Aristoxenes sought to develop the theory that the ear is the true judge of concord, and that its impressions may be generalized into rules. (See Class A, Ancient Greek Music.)

Asperges, (äs-pĕr'zĕz). An antiphon sung before the solemn mass on Sundays during which the priest sprinkles with holy water the altar and people.

Assai, (äs-sä'-ē). Very; as Allegro Assai, very quick.

Augmentation. A technical term signifying that a phrase is to be repeated with notes of double length.

Aulos, (ōw'-lŏs). The Greek flute; a sort of rude oboe.

Ave Regina, (ä-vĕh rä--jē-näh). "Hail Queen;" a hymn to the Virgin.

Barbiere di Siviglia, (bär-bē-ä-rĕ dĕ sē-bĕl-yä). "The Barber of Seville," a comic opera by Rossini, 1816.

Bard, (bärd). A poet and singer; one whose occupation was to compose and sing verses generally to the accompaniment of some stringed instrument.

Bardi, Giovanni. (jē-o-van'-nē bär'-dē). A Florentine patrician at whose palace Peri, Caccini, Renuccini and others met to study the Greek drama which resulted in the origin of the opera. (See Class C, *Eurydice*).

Ballet, (bäl'lä). A spectacular dance in which a number of performers take part.

Benediction des Poignards, (bĕn-ē-dik-shŏn duh pwoin-yärd). "Blessing of the Swords." Name of a very effective concerted piece in Meyerbeer's "Les Huguenots."

Benedictus, (bĕn-ē-dik'-tus). One of the principal movements of a mass.

Beni Hassan. (bĕn'-ī häs'-sän). One of the oldest burying places of the Egyptians.

Biban el Moulouk. (be-ban'-el-moo-look'). The ancient burial place of the kings in Egypt. Here were found illustrations of musical instruments.

Biber, H. J. F. von. (bē'-bar); b. Warthenberg in Bohemia, 1638; d. 1698. One of the finest violinists of his time His compositions were fanciful and beautiful. He was chapel master to Bishop of Salzburg.

Birde. English composers of the 17th century.

Bizet, G., (bē'-zä); b. Paris, 1838; d. 1875. One of the most distinguished of modern French composers. His most celebrated opera is "Carmen," which has long held a prominent place upon the operatic stage in both Europe and America, and still maintains its popularity.

Boyce, Wm.; b. London, 1710; d. 1779. A composer of ecclesiastical, dramatic and miscellaneous music of originality and of strong, clear style. In 1749 made Doctor of Music by Cambridge University. Published collection of standard works, by which England's choral service was much enriched.

Cadenza, (kä-dĕnt'-sä). A bravoura passage, commonly introduced toward the close of a piece. The most elaborate and difficult cadenzas are to be found in concertos.

Campenalla, (käm-pä-nĕl'-lä). A little bell.

Canon, (kăn'-ŏn). A composition in which a second voice repeats the first exactly, beginning later. This imitation may be in the unison, octave or any other interval. The second may also repeat the first backward, or inverse order of intervals, etc., in great variety.

Cantabile, (kän-tä'-bē-lĕ). In singing style. Cantando has the same meaning. Both are derived from the verb *cantare*, to sing.

Caccini, G. (kät-tshē'-nē); b. Rome, 1558; d. 1615. Noted scholar and dramatic composer; with J. Peri composed opera Eurydice. See Class C, Eurydice.

Cantata, (kän-tä'-tä). A composition generally elaborate for solos and chorus with or without orchestra. It is usually founded upon a connected story but without action. It is the secular counterpart of the oratorio.

Cantelena, (kän-tĭ-lä'-nä). A short lyric piece either for voice or instrument.

Cantillation. Chanting, recitation with musical modulations.

Cantiones Sacræ, (cän-tē-o'-nĕs sä'-crä). Sacred songs; a collection of motettes by Tallis and Bird. 1575.

Cantus Fermus, (kän'-tus fĭr'-mus). The fixed song, that is, the melody which is taken for treatment in counterpoint.

Canzona, (känt-so'-nä). A secular polyphonic song of popular character, peculiar to the 15th and 16th centuries. The corresponding French word is Chanson.

Catch. A humorous composition for three or four voices. Of English origin. The parts are so written that the singers catch up each others words giving them a different sense than that of the original reading.

Cenerentola, (tchĕn'-ĕr-ĕn-to'-lä). An opera by Rossini, written in 1817.

Cervantes, (sĕr-vän'-tĕz); b. 1547; d. 1616. The author of Don Quixote.

Chanson, (shänh-sŏnh). A little song; romances sung by minstrels of the middle ages. (See Class I, Definition of Qualities and Characterization of Song).

Chanson of Antioch. A celebrated romance or series of metrical romances relating the incidents of the siege of Antioch in the crusades. Developed in the middle ages, and very popular with all the minstrels for about two centuries.

Chanson of Roland. A mediaeval romance, or series of romances devoted to the story of Roland, a Knight in the suite of Charlemagne.

Chamisso, (shä-mis'-o); b. 1781; d, 1838. A German lyric poet. Author of the text to which Schumann set his beautiful music, "Woman's Love and Life."

Chevey Chase, (tschev'-y). An old English ballad.

Cherubini, (kĕr-ū-bē'-nē); b Florence, 1760; d. 1842. Eminent Italian composer of operas.

Chorale, (ko-rä-lĕ). Hymn tunes. The term properly applies to the German melodies sung by the Protestant congregations.

Chromatic Progressions. Progressions, or successions of chords, in which are introduced chromatic tones and chords not essentially belonging to the diatonic "track of the key."

Chromatic Passage. A brilliant passage of cadenza style, involving a large proportion of chromatic tones.

Chromatic Fantasia. A celebrated piece of music by John Sebastian Bach, for pianoforte. It is very free in style, and contains a long succession of very dramatic recitatives for instrument only, each phrase ending in a chord of the diminished seventh.

Claronet. Instrument of 4ft. tone consisting of a mouthpiece containing a single beating reed, a clyindrical tube terminating in a bell and eighteen openings, half closed by the fingers and other half by keys. Invented by Denner, at Nuremburg, 1690; improved by Klose of Vienna, 1843.

Clavier, or Clavichord. A small keyed instrument, like the spinet and the forerunner of the pianoforte.

Coda. (ko'-dä). An appendix; measures, phrases or passages added to form a more complete and satisfactory close.

Concertante. (kont-shĕr-täu'-tē). In the style of a concerto: concerted with other instruments.

Concerto. (kont-shär'-to). A composition (usually in sonata form) written for displaying a solo instrument, with orchestral accompaniment. (See Class F).

Consonance. Two tones satisfactory in combination. Consonance is the pleasing effect produced upon the ear by the perception that two tones sounding together have a principle of unity. The most perfect consonance is the octave, next the fifth and fourth (both perfect); thirds and sixths are classed as "imperfect" consonances in musical theory

Content. According to Mr. W. S. B. Matthews' definition, the content of a piece of music is the total impression it leaves upon the most congenial bearer or all the author has put into it, technical knowledge and skill, imagination and feeling.

Contrapuntal. (kŏn-trä-pun'-tl). Relating to counterpoint.

Correlli, A. (ko-rĕl'-lē): b. 1652; d. 1713. Greatest violin player of his time. He laid the foundation of the future development of technic. His compositions advanced the use of the violin as a solo and also as an orchestral instrument. One of the first actual virtuosi upon the violin and the founder of the free style of instrumental and orchestral compositions.

Counterpoint. The art of writing two or more voice-parts to proceed simultaneously. Double counterpoint is the art of writing two parts so that they will be correct when inverted. The idea of counterpoint involves melodic individuality in the added voice, and a flowing melodic motion. Counterpoint in its fullest extent is equivalent to a complete art of melodic invention.

Cramer, J. B. (crä'-mĕr); b. 1771; d. 1858. One of the principle founders of the modern pianoforte school. A prolific composer known now mainly for his "studies."

Credo. (krä'-do). I *believe;* one of the five principal movements of the mass.

Crucifixus. (krä-sĭ-fĭx'-us). Part of the *Credo* in a mass.

Cum Sancto Spiritu. (kŭm sank'-to spĭr-ĭ-tū). Part of the Gloria in a mass.

Czerny, (tschár'-nĭ); b. 1791; d. 1857. Prominent pianoforte teacher and composer in Vienna, chiefly celebrated for his famous "studies" which are now rapidly falling into disuse.

Dance Macabre, (dance mä-kä'-br). Dance of death. The title of a famous symphony by Saint-Saens. (See Class E.)

Da Ponte Lorenzo, (lo-rěnd-zo dä pŏn'-tä). An Italian poet, born at Ceneda, Venetian states, in 1749. Having been exiled from Venice for speaking disrespectfully of the republic, he went to Vienna, where he became librettist of Mozart, writing three operas, "Figaro," "Cosi fan Tutti" and "Don Giovanni." Died in New York, 1838.

De Capo, (dä kä'-po). From the beginning.

Des Prez, Josquin (zho'känh dŭp-prĕ'). See Class B.

Deucalion and Pyrrha. Deucalion and his wife Pyrrha, according to the Thessalian legend were the sole survivors of the deluge. To re-people the land, by command of the oracle, they threw behind them stones, which immediately turned into men and women.

Diapason, (dī-a-pā'-son). Greek term meaning "through the octave," used now in France to mean "standard of pitch." The English use it to name the fundamental stops of the organ. The diapason tone of the organ is a broad, solid, dignified tone quality, due to the pipes producing it being of a large diameter and liberally supplied with wind, the harmonics or upper partials, also, must be well represented.

Dies Iræ, (dī'-äz ĕ'-rä). A principal movement in a Requiem.

Die letzen Dinge, (dee lets'-zěn ding'-gĕ). "The Last Things." German name of an oratorio by Spohr. In English, commonly called "The Last Judgment."

Dissonance. A discord; an interval or chord displeasing to the ear and requiring to be followed by another chord in which the dissonant note is resolved.

Dolphin. A fish celebrated for its surprising changes of color when dying.

Dominant Seventh. A chord composed of the tones 5, 7, 9 and 11 of the key; called dominant because founded upon the fifth of the key; and "seventh" because in addition to a triad it has also the seventh from the root.

Dona Nobis. (do-nä no'-bis). The closing movement of the mass.

Dorian, (do'-rĕ-an). The name of one of the ancient modes or scales.

Dowland, J. An English composer and musician, author of many books and songs.

Dufay, (dü'-fâ). See Class B.

Elizabethan Age. Pertaining to England during the reign of Queen Elizabeth from 1558 to 1603.

Episode. An incidental narrative or digression. A portion of a composition not founded upon the principal subject or theme.

Ernani, (ĕr-nä'-nē). Italian opera founded upon Hugo's novel. Music by Verdi, Venice, March, 1844.

Et Incarnatus, (ĕt ın-kär-nä'-tus). A part of the Credo.

Et Resurrexit, (ĕt rĕs-ur-ĕx'ıt). One of the parts of the Credo.

Etude, (a'-tūd). A "study." See Etude, unclassified general card.

Euripides, (zoo-rıp'-ı-dĕz). Athenian tragic poet. See Class A, Ancient Greek Music.

Field, John; b. Dublin, 1784; d. 1837. A brilliant pianist and justly celebrated as the inventor of the "nocturne."

Finale, (fĕ-nä'-lĕ). The closing movement of an extended work; as a sonata, symphony, act of an opera, etc.

Flageolet. The modern form of the old straight flute.

Folk-song. A song of the people.

Gewandhaus, (gĕ-vänd'-hows). Gewandhaus concerts. These celebrated concerts originated with "das grosze concert" at the time when Bach was Cantor of the St. Thomas School at Leipsic. The Gewandhaus proper was established by Hiller. They consist of twenty winter concerts and two benefit concerts. There is a conductor and twelve directors, the orchestra numbering seventy performers.

Glee, a vocal composition in three or more parts; a part song. English.

Glinka, (glın'-kä). Novospaskoi, 1803-1857. A Russian composer whose two operas are considered as of national importance. They were among the first and best of Russian operas. They were, "A Life for the Czar," 1836; "Russian and Ludmilla," 1837.

Gloria, (glo'-rı-ä). One of the principal movements of a mass.

Gradus ad Parnassum, (grä'₂dus äd pär-näs'-sum). Road to Parnassus. Title of some text books and collection of etudes.

Gratius Agimus, (grä'-shĕ-as aj'-ĭ-mus). Part of the Gloria in a mass.

Grazioso, (grät-sĕ-o'-so). Gracefully.

Gregorian. Of or pertaining to St. Gregory the Great. He established the four "plagal" scales or "modes," and the "tones" or chants ever since called by his name.

Gurlitt, C.; b. 1818, at Altona. Author of compositions for male chorus, piano pieces and operas. Best known as composer of poetic pieces for piano.

Harmonics. Undertones. The tone produced by the fractions of a string or other vibrating body.

Harpsichord. An instrument similar to the pianoforte, except that the strings were plucked by means of quills instead of being struck by hammers. Invented 1600 or earlier. Went out of use about 1800.

Hebrides, (hĕb'-rĭ-dĕz). Name commonly applied to Mendelssohn's concert overture to Fingal's Cave in B minor, (op. 26), which he wrote in 1829, after a visit to the north of Scotland.

Hegel, (hā'-gĕl). Eminent German philosopher. Celebrated in music for his admirable works upon art and æthetics.

Homophony. Unison; one or more voices singing in unison.

Hosanna, (ho-zän'-nä). Part of the Sanctus in a mass.

Hummel, J. N. (hŭm'-mĕl); b. 1778; d. 1837. A celebrated pianist and composer.

Hyblian, (hi-blē'-ăn). Pertaining to Hybla, an ancient city in Sicily, celebrated for the honey produced on the neighboring hills.

Il Trovatore, (ēl trō'-vä-tō'-rĕh). The Troubadour. Celebrated opera by Verdi, Rome 1853.

Imitation. The repetition of a phrase or subject.

Imitation, Strict. An exact repetition or slightly modified repetition according to certain rules as exemplified in Canon and Fugue.

Improvisation. The act of singing, playing or composing music without previous preparation.

Intermezzo, (in-tĕr-mĕt'-so.) Interlude or detached piece, often a dance played between the acts of a drama. Used by Schumann and others for short pieces in a series having the character of interlude pieces.

Interlude. A composition played between two important members of a composition.

Kithara, (kıth'-a-rä). The lute; an old instrument of the guitar kind.

Koehler, Louis, (kā'-lér); b Brunswick, 1820. Musical director at Königsburg. Celebrated as a piano teacher; editor and writer of educational works.

Kreisleriana, (krīs'-lĕr ı-än'-ä). A set of eight pieces for piano solo by Schumann (op. 16) dedicated to Chopin.

Kuhnau, J. (koo'-now) Geysing, 1667-1722. A remarkable musician who became musical director of Leipsic University and conductor of St. Thomas School. Invented the sonata as a piece in several movements, wrote dance tunes and was the greatest composer for Harpischord up to Bach.

La Gazza Ladra, (lä gäts'-sä lä-drä'). "The Thieving Magpie," opera by Rossini, libretto Gherardini, produced at Milan, 1817.

Lamartine, (lä-mär-tēn'). A brilliant French writer. B. 1792; d. 1869. Noted as poet, historian and statesman.

Lassus, Orlando, (ŏr-län'-do läs'-sus). See Class B.

La Traviata, (lä trö'-vē-ä'-tä). An opera by Verdi produced at Venice, March 1853.

L' Homne Arme, (lom-är-mä'). "The Armed Man," the name of an old French Chanson the melody of which was used by many of the Netherlandish masters as subject for movements in masses and other compositions.

Libera Me, (lĕ'-bä-rä mä). "Deliver me, O Lord," one of the hymns from the Roman Catholic *Responsorium* used at the end of the Requiem mass on solemn occasions.

Litolff, H. C., (lıt'-ŏlf); b. London, 1818. Pupil of Moscheles and eminent pianist and composer.

Loeschhorn, A , (lāsh'-ŏrn); b. Berlin, 1819. Pianoforte professor in Berlin. Author of many valuable and well known etudes.

Lohengrin. Three act dramatic opera by Wagner. Composed in 1847 and produced at Weimar by Liszt in 1850.

Magnificato, (măg-nĭf-ē-cä'-to). Part of the evening service of the Catholic Church.

Marbecke, J.; d. 1585. Adapted old plain song of Latin services to English book of common prayer.

Meeressille. Calm at Sea and Prosperous Voyage, poem by Goethe. See Manual of Music, p. 358, revised edition.

Mensural. Applied especially to music to which measure was applied. See Class B.

Mephistopheles, (mĕf-ĭs-tŏf'-ē lēz). The Devil. Name applied to the Satanic character in Goethe's Faust.

Midsummer's Night's Dream. Music for this play by Mendelssohn. (1) An overture, 1827; (2) Twelve numbers produced by command of the King of Prussia, 1843.

Millais, John E. (mĭl-lā'). An English painter.

Modal. (mo'-dal). Pertaining to mode or mood; relating to form. Having the form without the essence or reality.

Monody, (mon'-o-dy). A composition upon one subject.

Monothetic, (mŏn-o-thĕt'-ĭc). Implying a single essential element.

Monophony, (mŏn'-o-fo-ni). Same as monody.

Motive A short fragment of melody usually one measure in length used as a pattern, model, design.

Morley, Thomas. Pupil of Bird in 16th century. Noted English composer.

Motet. A short vocal composition for church use; nearly equivalent to anthem.

Mueller, Max, (mĕl'-lĕr). German-English Sanscript scholar.

Neri, San Phillippo, (nā'-rē). Italian founder of the society "Priests of the Oratory."

Node. Point of division in a string when it is vibrating in fractions.

Notation. The manner of representing to the eye. Musical notation comprises lines and spaces representing scale degrees, the clefs determining the absolute pitch intended by the lines and spaces, notes indicating the number of musical utterances required, and by their forms the relative length of utterance.

Oboe, (ho'-bo). A modern reed instrument of two-foot tone borrowing one or two semitones from the octave above. It is played with a double reed.

Offertorio, (ŏf-fĕr-to'-rē-o). A hymn, anthem or instrumental piece sung or played during the collection of the offertory.

Offertorium. Same as Offertorio.

Okegham, (o'-kä-ghĕm). See Class B.

Opus, (o'-pus). Work. Used to number the published works of a composer in the order of publication, as Op.1, Op.2, etc.

Overture. A piece introducing an opera or play. Usually in sonata form, and generally intended to foreshadow the emotional contents of what is to follow.

Palestrina, (päl-ä-strĕ'-nä). See Class B.

Phorminx, (fŏr'-mĭnx). A lyre.

Pianissimo, (pē-än-ĕs'-sē-mo). Extremely soft.

Pizzcato, (pĕt-sē-kä' to). Pinched. A direction to pick the strings of a violin, etc. with the fingers, producing a staccato effect.

Plagal Cadence. Applied to the close made by the under-fifth (sub-dominant) chord followed by the tonic.

Plagal Modes. Opposed to "authentic." Ancient church modes or scales running from under-fifth of the "authentic" modes.

Polyphony, (po'-lĭf-o-ni). "Many sounds." Used of music with two or more independent voice parts or melodies proceeding simultaneously.

Polythetic. Plurality of parts.

Pot-pourri, (pŏt-poor-rē). A medley.

Prelude, (prĕ'-lūde). A preparatory passage or movement intended to lead to something else.

Presto, (pres'-to) Quick, rapid.

Programme-music. Music intended to express the succession of emotions suitable to the successive incidents of a story, and perhaps also to suggest those incidents

Ptolemy, Claudius, (tŏl'-ĕ-mi). Greek-Egyptian astronomer and geometer. Was also a learned theorist in the mathematics of music. In his "Harmonik" he gives a summary of all the Greek learning upon this subject. Lived at Alexandria about 200 B. C.

Purcell, H.; 1658–1692. English composer of songs, overtures and operas, and chamber music of great merit. Did much to advance and elevate art in England.

Rebec. A Moorish word signifying an instrument with two strings, played with a bow.

Recitative, (rĕ-sĭ-tä-tēv'). See Characterization of Opera, Class C.

Reinecke, Karl, (rīn'-ĕk-ē); b. 1824. Eminent German performer, conductor and composer.

Rigoletti, (rē-go-lä'-to). Opera by Verdi.

Rinuccini, (rē-noo-tschē'-nē). Wrote the words of Eurydice, the first opera.

Rondo, (rŏn'-do). A round; piece in which the principal theme constantly reappears with connected links between the repetitions.

Round. A species of canon in the unison or octave, also a vocal composition in three or more parts, all written in the same clef, the performers singing each part in succession.

Sanctus, (sănk'-tŭs). Holy. One of the principal movements of the mass.

Semirade, (sä-mē-rä'-děh). Opera by Rossini, Venice, 1823.

Scherzo, (skärt'-so). Play; sport; jest.

Schmitt, Aloys, (shmĭt); 1789–1866. Distinguished as a pianoforte teacher and as a voluminous writer of studies and pieces for his instrument.

Sixtette. A composition introducing six voices.

Saloman Symphonies. A series of twelve symphonies composed by Haydn, and first introduced at Philharmonic concerts, London.

Sonare, (so-nä'-rĕ). To sound.

Sophocles, (sŏf'-o-klīz). Greek tragic poet.

Stabat-Mater, (stä'-bat mät'-tĕr). "The mother stood." A hymn on the Crucifix.

Stretta, (strät'-tä). Concluding passage taken in quicker time to enhance the effect.

Suite, (sweet). A series of pieces to be played in connection. The suites of Bach and Handel had six or eight pieces, all in the same key, and contrasted in tempo and character.

Sussēmeyer, F., (süs'-mī-ĕr): 1766–1803. Director and composer to National Theatre, Vienna, 1795. Friend of Mozart and composer of operas, etc.

Tallis, Thomas. Court organist to Henry VIII; d. 1585. The greatest benefactor of English church music. One of the greatest contrapuntists.

Tartini, G., (tär-tē'-nē); 1692–1770. Leading violinist of his time. Founded a violin school and new system of harmony.

Tarantelle, (tär-än-tä'-lĕ). A whirling, swift Neapolitan dance in 6-8 time.

Tausig, C., (tow'-sĭg); 1841–1871. Pupil of Liszt, and one of the very greatest pianists.

Te Deum Laudamus, (tĕ-dĭ'-um lau'-dä-mus). We praise Thee. A hymn of praise.

Timbre, (tămhbr). Quality of tone or sound

Tonic-triad. A triad on the tonic or fundamental tone in the major or minor.

Triplet. A group of three notes played in the usual time of two similar ones.

Troubadour. A bard and poet-musician of the middle ages.

Tschaikowsky, Peter, (tschi-koff'-ski); b. 1840. Prominent Russian composer of the modern school.

Tutti, (toot'-tē). All the strings.

Veda. The ancient sacred literature of the Hindoos.

Vikings. The pirate chiefs from among the Northmen, who plundered the coasts of Europe during the 8th and 9th centuries.

Virtuoso, (vĕr-too-o'-zo). A masterly performer

Willaert, Adrian, (vĭl-lärt'). See Class B.

Weelkes, Thomas. Organist of Winchester and author of madrigals printed in 1597.

Zarlino, G., (tsär-lē-no); 1517–1590. Organist and director at Saint Marks, at Venice. Distinguished as a theorist and composer.

GENERAL INDEX.

		Page
AMBROSE, ST., Early Ecclesiastical Music	Reg.	23
	Nor.	96
Ancient Egyptian Music	Reg.	13
	Nor.	95
Ancient Greek Music	Reg.	20
	Nor.	96
Ancient Hindoo Music	Reg.	18
	Nor.	95
BACH, C. P. E.,		
Sonata in F Minor	Reg.	68
	Nor.	112
BACH, J. S.,		
Oratorio, Passion Music	Reg.	44
	Nor.	104
BEETHOVEN, LUDWIG VAN,		
Concerto, "Emperor" E Flat op. 73	Reg.	57
	Nor.	110
Opera, Fidelio	Reg.	37
	Nor.	102
Oratorio, Mount of Olives	Reg.	47
	Nor.	105
Quartet, E Flat op. 131	Reg.	72
	Nor.	115
Sonata, Appassionata	Reg.	66
	Nor.	113
Song, Adelaide	Reg.	78
	Nor.	118
Symphony, Fifth in C Minor	Reg.	51
	Nor.	108
BISHOP, SIR HENRY,		
Song, Home Sweet Home	Reg.	76
	Nor.	119
BRAHMS, JOHANNES,		
Quartet in C Minor	Reg.	71
	Nor.	116
CAVALIERE, EMILIO DEL,		
Oratorio, Representation of the Soul and Body	Reg.	45
	Nor.	104
Chamber Music, Definition of Qualities and Characterization	Reg.	70
	Nor.	115

INDEX.

		Page
CHOPIN, FREDERIC,		
Concerto in E minor op. 11	Reg. Course.	58
	Nor. "	111
Classical in Music. The	Reg. "	86
	Nor. "	120
Concerto, Definition of Qualities and Characterization	Reg. "	56
	Nor. "	110
Definition of Music. Its beginnings	Reg. "	11
	Nor. "	93
DONIZETTI, GAETANO,		
Opera, Lucia di Lammermoor	Reg. "	39
	Nor. "	103
Dufay and Early Polyphony	Reg. "	28
	Nor. "	97
Early Christian Music, Distinctive Character of	Reg. "	23
	Nor. "	96
Etude, Qualities of	Reg. "	81
	Nor. "	122
Fantasia	Reg. "	81
	Nor. "	121
FAURE, J. P.		
Song, Palm Branches	Reg. "	79
	Nor. "	119
Franco of Cologne and Franco of Paris	Reg. "	27
	Nor. "	97
Fugue, The	Reg. "	88
	Nor. "	121
GLUCK, CHRISTOPHER,		
Opera, Orpheus,	Reg. "	36
	Nor. "	101
GOUNOD, CHARLES,		
Opera, Faust	Reg. "	40
	Nor. "	103
Gregory the Great, St., and his Reforms	Reg. "	24
	Nor. "	96
GRIEG, EDWARD,		
Quartet for Strings, G Minor	Reg. "	73
	Nor. "	117
Guido, Solmization and Staff	Reg. "	26
	Nor. "	97
HAYDN, FRANCES JOSEPH,		
Oratorio, Creation	Reg "	45
	Nor "	105
Sonata in E Flat	Reg. "	64
	Nor. "	112
Symphony, "Oxford"	Reg. "	54
	Nor. "	107

INDEX.

HANDEL, G. F.,			Page.
Oratorio, Messiah...	Reg.	Course.	44
	Nor.	"	105
History of Music; Reasons why it should be	Reg.	"	84
Studied	Nor.	"	120
Hucbald, Diaphony, Organum and Notation.	Reg.	"	23
	Nor.	"	97
INSTRUCTIONS			125
CLASSIFICATION OF CARDS. { Specific Cards			125
Classified General Cards			125
Unclassified General Cards			126
How Books are Composed			126
Value of Books			127
How to Acquire the Cards			129
Requirements of the Progressive Grades			131
Normal Course (Instructions.)			153
Normal Course (Questions.)			93
Supplementary Rules and Suggestions			160
LASSUS, ORLANDO, and His Place in Art	Reg.	"	30
	Nor.	"	99
LISZT, FRANZ.			
Concerto: First in E Flat major	Reg.	"	61
	Nor.	"	111
Symphony, Les Preludes	Reg.	"	54
	Nor.	"	108
Literary Interpretation in Musical Æsthetics	Reg.	"	89
	Nor.	"	120
LULLI, J. B.,			
Opera, Armide	Reg.	"	35
	Nor.	"	101
LUTHER, MARTIN, and the Protestant Chorale.	Reg.	"	30
	Nor.	"	98
Madrigal, and its Related Part Songs, The,	Reg.	"	85
	Nor.	"	122
Mass	Reg.	"	91
	Nor.	"	122
MATTEI, TITO,			
Song, Non e Ver	Reg.	"	77
	Nor.	"	118
Mediæval Secular Music	Reg.	"	26
	Nor.	"	98
MENDELSSOHN, FELIX,			
Concerto in F Minor	Reg.	"	60
	Nor.	"	111
Oratorio, Elijah	Reg.	"	46
	Nor.	"	105
Symphony, Scotch in A Minor op. 56..	Reg.	"	51
	Nor.	"	108
MEYERBEER, GIACOMO,			
Opera, The Huguenots	Reg.	"	39
	Nor.	"	102

INDEX.

			Page.
MONTEVERDE, C.,			
Opera, Tancredi	Reg.	Course.	35
	Nor.	"	100
MOZART, WOLFGANG,			
Opera, Don Giovanni	Reg.	"	37
	Nor.	"	101
Sonata in C Minor	Reg.	"	65
	Nor.	"	113
Symphony, "Jupiter."	Reg.	"	50
	Nor.	"	107
Nocturne	Reg.	"	82
	Nor.	"	122
Okegham, Des Pres, Willaert and Gombert.	Reg.	"	29
	Nor.	"	98
Opera, Characterization of	Reg.	"	33
	Nor.	"	100
Opera, Definition of Qualities of	Reg.	"	33
	Nor.	"	100
Oratorio, Definition of Qualities and Characterization of	Reg.	"	42
	Nor.	"	104
PAGANINI, NICOLO,			
Concerto in E Minor	Reg.	"	62
	Nor.	"	110
PALESTRINA and Pure Church Music	Reg.	"	31
	Nor.	"	99
PERI, JACOPO,			
Opera, Eurydice	Reg.	"	34
	Nor.	"	100
Principles of the Beautiful, The	Reg.	"	92
	Nor.	"	124
Pronunciation, Key to	Reg.	"	93
	Nor.	"	124
Requiem	Reg.	"	87
	Nor.	"	123
Romantic, Definition of the	Reg.	"	90
	Nor.	"	124
ROSSINI, GIOACHINO,			
Opera, William Tell	Reg.	"	38
	Nor.	"	102
RUBINSTEIN, ANTON,			
Trio, B Flat Major op. 52	Reg.	"	70
	Nor.	"	116
SAINT-SAENS, CHARLES C.,			
Concerto in G Minor	Reg.	"	60
	Nor.	"	110
Quintet for Piano and Strings	Reg.	"	73
	Nor.	"	116
Symphony, Dance of Death	Reg.	"	53
	Nor.	"	109

		Page
SCARLATTI, A.,		
Opera. Teodora	Reg.	Course, 35
	Nor.	" 101
SCHUBERT, FRANZ.		
Quartet in D Minor	Reg.	" 74
	Nor.	" 115
Sonata in A Minor	Reg.	" 66
	Nor.	" 113
Song, Erl King	Reg.	" 76
	Nor.	" 118
Symphony in C Major	Reg.	" 52
	Nor.	" 108
SCHUMANN, ROBERT,		
Concerto in A Minor	Reg.	" 58
	Nor.	" 111
Quintet in E Flat	Reg.	" 74
	Nor.	" 116
Sonata in G Minor op. 22	Reg.	" 67
	Nor.	" 114
Song, He, the Noblest	Reg.	" 77
	Nor.	" 119
Sonata, Definition of Qualities and Characterization of	Reg.	" 63
	Nor.	" 112
Song, Definition of Qualities and Characterization of	Reg.	" 75
	Nor.	" 118
Song Without Words	Reg.	" 83
	Nor.	" 123
SPOHR, LUDWIG.		
Oratorio, Last Judgment	Reg.	" 47
	Nor.	" 106
SULLIVAN, SIR ARTHUR,		
Song, Lost Chord	Reg.	" 78
	Nor.	" 119
Symphony, Definition of Qualities and Characterization of	Reg.	" 49
	Nor.	" 107
Te Deum	Reg.	" 83
	Nor.	" 123
Typical Musical Forms	Reg.	" 80
	Nor.	" 121
VERDI, G.,		
Opera, Aida	Reg.	" 40
	Nor.	" 103
WAGNER, RICHARD,		
Opera, Tristan and Isolde	Reg.	" 41
	Nor.	" 103
WEBER CARL VON,		
Opera, Der Freischuetz	Reg.	" 38
	Nor.	" 102
Sonata in A Flat	Reg.	" 69
	Nor.	" 113

www.ingramcontent.com/pod-product-compliance
Lightning Source LLC
Chambersburg PA
CBHW020842160426
43192CB00007B/749